EBURY PRESS

# FIFTY TOUGHEST QUESTIONS OF LIFE

Deepak Ramola is the founder and artistic director of Project FUEL. He is currently pursuing a master's programme at the Harvard Graduate School of Education. A TED Talks speaker and UN Action Plan Executor, he previously served as the Kindness Ambassador for the UNESCO Mahatma Gandhi Institute of Education for Peace and Sustainable Development. His methodology has been recognized among the world's top 100 innovations in education by the Finland-based organization HundrED and has been adopted across five continents. Ramola is also a celebrated lyricist in Hindi cinema, and his songs have been voiced by Amitabh Bachchan, Farhan Akhtar and Rekha Bhardwaj, among others. His first collection of Hindi poetry, *Itna Toh Main Samajh Gaya Hoon*, received the prestigious Dwarka Prasad Aggarwal Young Writer Award in 2020.

## PRAISE FOR THE BOOK

'Deepak Ramola is a poet and a sage, an artist and a truly deep thinker. Above all else, he has a unique ability to ask the most profound questions that never fail to elicit the most deeply authentic replies, because you instinctively know your thoughts are entirely safe in his hands. This curious humanitarian spreads love and lessons wherever he goes'—Juliet Blake, head of television, TED

'I'm ceaselessly amazed by the inspiring stories Deepak collects from around the world. Instilled into this lyrical book, they will move you to look within and become more compassionate. An incredible and important book for our times. Poetic, profound and purposeful'—Abhay Deol, actor and producer

'I first met Deepak Ramola in Bhutan many years back. He surprised me with his insight into everything and he carried an attitude surpassing his colleagues. I knew he would be somebody one day. If we honour his questions and ask them ourselves, we will be liberated. His book helps a reader realize that we may land in the most undesirable season of our lives, but it will pass meaningfully if we rightly know how to edit our lives. Reading through this book, you can hear the heart of a real-lifetime explorer in the uncharted universe. His book proposes that readers look for the crack in their lives where the light is passing from and cultivate it. He implores us to realize that people can awaken from a deep slumber by keeping belief and faith that seemingly travel endlessly to beyond life's journey. Success is not predesigned and measured by its owner, making friends with the self and churning the mind to its full potential gives the potion of immortality for the ultimate journey to life's end'—Dr Saamdu Chetri, PhD, visiting professor, Rekhi Centre of Excellence for the Science of Happiness, IIT Kharagpur

'I can imagine how challenging it would be to tackle fifty toughest questions of life, but Deepak Ramola did it with such finesse, and only a talented, kind and compassionate man like him possibly could. This book creates an understanding of reality and gives you a sense of hope. Deepak takes us on a journey where we learn about him and the challenges he faced since childhood and how he overcame them. He collected life lessons at the age of fourteen from people he met all over the globe. A must-read book written with such openness and honesty, kindness, compassion and hope, which will definitely challenge the way we think and in the process also learn valuable lessons from it'—Sundeep Bhutoria, trustee, Prabha Khaitan Foundation

# LOVE NOTES FROM READERS

'*Fifty Toughest Questions of Life* is definitely one of my best reads. It gave me just what I needed, self-introspection and zooming out, to understand and feel things which are otherwise neglected in this busy life. Also, it is really special to me as I discussed these questions with my boyfriend during our initial days, which led us to bond more and know each other better. Definitely a gift to give others and yourself too, if you are trying to reflect on your journey. The best part about this book is that you can read it each year and find yourself giving different answers each time'—Kritika Tripathi

'This book offers a kaleidoscope of perspectives, enough to convince me once again to pause, reflect and answer these questions once again. One who reflects [on] these questions will inspire, aspire and disentangle life'—Aadil Belim

'Even though I'm just fourteen, this book made me realize how we humans have the privilege to question everything around us, how we aren't bound. I still question everything around me! Each page has enlightened me. Truly amazing!'—Aanya Agarwal

'Thank you for the book and for making people come alive with the writing'—Aditya Ghodasara

'A warm hug after a bad day, home-cooked food's comfort, fresh wind on a late-night walk and happy childhood recollections are just a few examples of defining moments that can succinctly sum up my feelings about this book. This book provided me with a completely new understanding of what I yearned for. *Fifty Toughest Questions of Life* is nothing but my home away from home'—Mannavi Nehra

'The book is sunshine. To summarize: I have lived better ever since I read and [sought] the answers to the questions myself. To people who haven't read this, you're missing out on something hopeful, poetic, warm'—Aastha Gautam

'For someone who hasn't yet found the purpose of my life, this book has definitely helped me through the rollercoaster ride this world has been, with its unpredictable ways. This book offers simple introspection to the most common riddles of life, which many of us find hard giving or getting answers to. In the simplest way, for someone who is directionless and seeking answers to the many questions in their life: these fifty toughest questions will help them navigate and guide them through the ups and downs, as they look for hope and faith for their own existence in this universe'—Dhaval Bakshi

'I have read this book multiple times. Each time I read a chapter I draw something new from it. I get up early in the morning and read a chapter before my kids go off to school. It starts my day mindfully. I am continually surprised when I find something that seems so relevant to me at the time, that I had not focused on it before. It's almost as if the book evolves to meet me in the moment'—Lea Ann Lope

'My Dad and I both have read the book. He read it before me and advised me to keep reading it often. And when I did, I found a harmonious resonance between my own set of beliefs and the ones shared by Deepak in his book. I found myself feeling vulnerable without feeling weak. The book is a humble reminder of the soft joys in life, the tender power of love and the magic in having faith. Multiple readings are recommended, as few are not enough'—Sarvajit Tawade

'The book felt like the best kind of catch-up with a dear, honest companion. Some pages felt like mirror conversations, some helplessly true and most filled us with sparks of joy . . . We feel inspired to find our own versions of the right answers!'—Purkal Stree Shakti

# 50 *TOUGHEST QUESTIONS OF LIFE*

Deepak Ramola

EBURY
PRESS

An imprint of Penguin Random House

EBURY PRESS

USA | Canada | UK | Ireland | Australia
New Zealand | India | South Africa | China

Ebury Press is part of the Penguin Random House group of companies
whose addresses can be found at global.penguinrandomhouse.com

Published by Penguin Random House India Pvt. Ltd
4th Floor, Capital Tower 1, MG Road,
Gurugram 122 002, Haryana, India

First published in Ebury Press by Penguin Random House India 2020

Copyright © Deepak Ramola 2020

All rights reserved

10 9 8 7 6 5 4 3 2 1

ISBN 9780143451044

Typeset in Adobe Caslon Pro by Manipal Technologies Limited, Manipal

www.penguin.co.in

*To my soulkeepers,*
*Deepika and Apoorva*

# Contents

# Preface

As I stood by the self-help section of a quaint, street-side bookstore in San Francisco, my mind swam through books and books of a condensed understanding of life by the renowned philosophers and thought leaders of our times. Laced with poignant metaphors, moving imagery and stimulating quotes, for the first time, I was a bit lost and confused. I found myself enclosed in the safe barricades of answers upon answers. Each book I picked up had many more answers. My mind raced to think that if these are the answers then what are the questions? And even if we do know them, how often do we ask ourselves the hard ones?

The seed of this book was sown exactly there—as I stood in the third row from the left, at the first corner of the self-help section in the San Francisco bookstore. This wasn't the first time I had an epiphany about this, but I felt convinced and finally compelled to write this book and add meaning to our lives.

My journey with life-changing questions isn't a new one. For years, I have toiled and scavenged through conversations, books and the Internet to look for the difficult questions, or, to put it mildly, the 'thought-provoking questions' of life. After condensing nearly 3000 questions into a list of the top fifty, I designed this as an exercise and a game to play with diverse shades of people over the past five years. It was all inspired by a young girl from Afghanistan, who once said to me, 'Life isn't about giving easy answers but answering tough questions.' There began my quest to discover, curate and create life's toughest questions.

This book asks you those questions. Encourages you to acknowledge them. And hopefully, inspires you to sail towards answering them, one at a time. But don't feel intimidated or overwhelmed. With each question, I have made an effort to pack some reflections, anecdotes, experiences and personal notes to help you along your crusade. Take your time with each question. Return to the ones that resonate, and ruminate over the ones which you don't yet have an answer for.

I am offering a few seeds of reflection, and I hope they serve you in growing an orchard of self-wisdom. If you are not someone who enjoys being questioned, I hope the stories and personal notes following each chapter will enthral and engage you.

My hope is this: At the very end of this journey, as you lift your head from the very last page of this book and look up at the sky of your life, each answer will connect magically to reveal a beautiful constellation of learning.

I am keeping an eye out too, so that I don't miss it. In the meantime, sending the joy of vibrant sunsets, the comfort of meaningful conversations and soul-stirring moments of reflection your way.

Did you not
always know
you would
end up here?

I have never been surer of the 'I don't belong here' feeling than when I was preparing for the Indian Institute of Technology and electrical and electronics engineering exams. My house was an hour and a half away from school, and the coaching institute was somewhere midway between the two, so to save some effort, on most days, I would get off my school bus, dressed in my school uniform, and head straight to a four-hour mind marathon after a ten-hour school day. I was miserable. As miserable, emotionally and socially, as I can remember myself ever being. It was the trend and, in many ways, an unspoken norm, to be an engineering aspirant in my small home town of Dehradun. If you were a science student and a good one, not qualifying for a major entrance exam was unthinkable. So the peer pressure cooked me into signing up for it. And, because my parents had paid seventy thousand rupees in cash for a two-year subscription, I felt too guilty to bail out. So I kept at it every single evening for two years.

While most of my coaching mates would flash their intelligence every time the professor raised a question, I would doodle in the back pages of my notebook and dream about a life far away from this reality. I think the law of attraction works. Coupled with the courage to speak up, resilience and a non-negotiable amount of hard work, it does work. At least in my case it has. In these classes, I would think about travelling the world and talking to all kinds of people. I loved knowing people's stories, and would constantly think I could use my love for conversations and speak for a living. But who would talk to me? How would I make a living out of this? Was there an opportunity for me out there that did not need a network or high-profile connections?

My mind would dance unchoreographed amidst these questions, and yet my heart would invariably assure me that it would happen. I did not know at the time how and when, but I knew it would. And therefore, I would rehearse, engaging in imaginary interviews. I would pretend to be in an airplane seat, reading a book and writing a speech or a song's lyrics on my computer. I would scribble poetry in the footnotes sections of my journal as if it were a manuscript waiting to be published.

Years later, I *am* writing this reflection sitting in an airplane, with my poetry book right in front of me, in the front pocket of my seat, and I am returning from hosting a major conference in Mumbai where I had the honour of talking to a Nobel Peace Prize winner, a renowned world dancer and a fascinating neuroscientist, among other remarkable people with unique stories.

After two years of slogging at that coaching institute, I acknowledged that I was at the wrong place, at the wrong time and doing the wrong thing. And that never in my life would I allow all those three probabilities to align again. At the most, it would be just two of them, and that would be a huge success, having learnt my lessons from that experience.

We all are constructing our lives by laying the brick of one decision over another. It always helps to ponder whether or not your life today is a sum total of all the choices you have made so far. And whether or not you knew all along you'll end up exactly where you are.

If you could
design a menu
for your life,
what all would
it include?

E very time I ask someone this question, two things happen: First, a smile breaks out on their face, and second, they ask me to break it down further and explain.

It's quite simple, though: If you could curate a metaphoric menu for your life, what all would you include? What would brighten your breakfast, what would you have for lunch, what would dinner be, and, finally, what would dessert comprise of? You guessed right—I am not talking about food here.

I ask this question as an exercise to look for what is most important to you. What truly matters and what can you have more of?

Meaningful conversations, poetry, time with my kind of humans, writing or being in the back seat of a car, listening to a favourite music playlist—all these things soothe my soul. Therefore, the menu of my life would include some soulful personal time at the start of the day, lunch would comprise conversations with people I love, dinner would be peppered with poetry recitals, and dessert would sweeten the deal with a long solitary walk or a quick drive on empty roads with a loved one.

Swimming in the morning, sunbathing, drinking a cup of tea with my grandfather, reading a nice book, meditating, taking short naps, long walks, cooking for the family, daydreaming, playing a game of cards, writing letters, receiving handwritten letters, chatting with my partner, wine tasting, hanging out with friends, watching a gripping movie on the Internet—these are the responses I get from people when I ask them what is on their life's menu.

Only when you filter the best in your life, take note of its worthiness, can you truly encourage yourself to let go of what doesn't serve you any more, or as Marie Kondo, the Japanese tidying expert, says 'doesn't spark joy in you'. The question of deciding your menu is an act of gratitude for what exists, and it helps you realize that certain nights should be full of more than the usual. Some days leave you only when you hum your favourite songs as a lullaby or let an old tune fill up the silence. Or you reflect back to the glory of old memories with close ones in full force. A conventional curation runs the risk of making a new 'hello' taste drab in the mouth of adventure, while 'goodbyes' will undermine the potential of all that you should hold on to. So think aloud and wild.

You know, if I could sit down with you in a café that has white wooden chairs, green walls and small plants cupped in recycled glass bottles, I would tell you that the universe is ready to deliver. It's you who hasn't placed the order as yet. And to do so, you often have to ask for a menu or create your own. Weigh your options, see through your choices. You are worthy of being coddled. So sit back in a sunlit patch of your room. Unbutton your happiness. Create your menu. This time!

Your heart, my love, is hungry.

## 3

Does the
world offend
you or amaze
you?

A n old memory visits me.

As we walked down the touristy path on our way back from the Mayan ruins in Tulum, Mexico, Ale pointed out two trees that looked strikingly identical. 'One is called "Chechém",' said Ale, 'and the other is "Chaka". One is poisonous and the other is its antidote. They both grow together.' 'How poetic is that?' I thought.

I often think about that day and those trees with smiling nostalgia. There is something peculiar about that fact that has stayed with me. Sure enough there is.

As that incident revisits my memory, I take a moment to dig in and read up about those trees on the Internet. I stumble upon a blog by the writer John Peck about this beautiful folklore, explaining why Chechém and Chaka grow close to one another. It comes from an oral tradition handed down through history in Yucatec Maya. It goes like this.

Once upon a time, there were two ancient brothers, Kinch and Tizic, young Mayan lords who fell tragically in love with the same beautiful woman, Nicté-Ha. The brothers were polar opposites; one calm and thoughtful, the other reckless and evil. They fought a furious battle driven by passionate jealousy, and, in the end, died in each other's arms, neither attaining the love they so endlessly sought. Their final request

13

to the gods was to see their beloved Nicté-Ha again, so the brothers were reincarnated as Chechém and Chaka—two trees that share one flower.

The legend is actually an obscure clue to the puzzle of the trees. The answer has to do with the flowers and fruit both these trees produce. It turns out that by 'sharing the same flower' (and fruit), these trees also end up sharing various birds that typically eat from them. The seeds are then deposited in the same place and often take root less than a metre apart.

As I share this with my mother, she tells me about *bichu ghass*, a thorny plant which upon touching can make your body itch like a monkey. But right beside it is its cure. She subtly hints that everyone who mistakenly or intentionally gets the bichu sting starts to run away from the plant due to the anxiety, stress and panic caused by the itch, unaware that the cure is right there. Such 'sting and relief' relationships are actually quite common in nature.

I think this stands true for most of our problems too. Our 'Chaka' is close by, waiting to catch our attention.

There is something reassuringly cathartic about these stories. I cannot fully point out what, but I know for sure it exists.

## 4

If love is
the answer,
what is the
question?

I think I know mine. 'What is something you can attempt over and over and never fail at?' LOVE!

Love cannot be a failure. To be capable of love cannot be your weakness. If someone argues over this to convince you otherwise, don't fight back. Give them time to find their way to the truth. They deserve to be lost in the moment, in the confusion about the reality of what it means to be truly, genuinely loved. Because they will grow and mature and heal and evolve to decipher that just because the world did not offer it to them appropriately the first time, it does not mean that they don't deserve it the second time. In fact, they—more than anyone else—are worthy of it.

To experience such love is to be baptized with a privilege. What a luxury it is to experience true love in this lifetime. To be completely cherished by another human being for who you are, or to cherish someone yourself. Embraced with your scars and accepted for your shortcomings. Try not to lose your head when that love finds you. And if you do, get back to it as soon as you knock some sense into your brain. What have you earned in this world really, if not the genuine love of someone—sacred, pristine and magnificent?

Along the way, be aware of people who harden you in the name of love; it's easy to mistake this as possessiveness. Real love softens you, till you dissolve into your own happiness. It allows you to absorb others into your world and expand if need be, like the universe. Not stand up like a wall and demand everything to hit you hard before it can belong to you. Be cautious of people who try to convince you otherwise. No hammer has ever helped a flower bloom.

Some people responded to the question 'If love is the answer, what is the question?' with 'What is something you can live without but shouldn't?' and 'What comforts and scares you at the same time?'

All of them agreed that to find and experience true love is like seeing a shooting star. No amount of fame, wealth, accolades or power can construct the magic of witnessing a shooting star. That moment of serendipity is a pure concoction of giving in to hope, looking up at the larger universe with belief, and waiting patiently. And if you are fortunate, that's where it happens. A lightning strike, travelling through breathing galaxies and uncovering your attention to fulfil a wish that you deeply want to come true.

## 5

Who would
you want
to be a witness
to your
life?

If there is anyone who has truly and consistently been my soulkeeper, friend, mentor, guide, soundboard, admirer, cheerleader and truth-teller, it is Apoorva Bakshi.

Over the years, I have attempted multiple times, in many ways, to describe what Apoorva means to me. Each year, through a birthday message or a random appreciation post, I try to word my emotions. Here are some ways in which I have expressed it over the years:

> Some people are a beacon of light, no matter where they are or who they become. They outstretch their shoulders to strengthen and support us so we can rise. They lay out a legacy carpet for us to walk on. They take the brick and share the cake.
>
> I wonder what it is about you that every time they try to dissolve you, you shine like glitter. I wonder what it is about you that every time they question your capacity to love, instead of shrinking, you expand a bit more. I wonder what it is about you that every time they call you names, you respond with your definition. I wonder what it is about you that the harshness of the world hasn't been able to harm you; the complexities haven't been able to overpower your calm; the pain hasn't perturbed your being; their

scarcity hasn't diminished your abundance. I wonder what is it about you that makes you win over their insecurities. I wonder what it is about you that you bloom, despite it all. I wonder. I wonder. I wonder.

And she is not a flower. Swaying with the wind, caressed by the gentle touches of a fragrance that emerges out of a transitory inheritance. She is instead a forest. Wild with its own chase; of all the possibilities it holds within. Carved by the depth of its existence and in awe of its own legacy.

You seem all flesh and bones from the outside, but I am convinced that you are made of silent prayers, rare gift wraps, bear hugs and twenty-four-carat love! I am constantly amazed by your ability to hold space for everyone, to see life in full colour, to find a reason to make the best of this imperfect world. You are my rock, my river and my tree. Happiest birthday, my love, your aura keeps the world warm.

Broken bones, mighty heart! There is a quality in people who are here to stay. They don't hand out excuses on street corners and do not blame you for being a slow learner. They show up on good days, and definitely make it a point to show up on bad ones too. They can call in sick but don't. Rather, they give 110 per cent of themselves when they possibly cannot. And by 'they', I mean Apoorva Bakshi.

These are just half my emotions, and I am not even close to capturing the entirety of this powerhouse. For those of you wondering who Apoorva Bakshi is, let me share this with you: When a seventeen-year-old boy is being laughed at for collecting and teaching life lessons, people like Apoorva Bakshi save their confidence so they can go on to build movements like Project FUEL. She is the daughter of my Hindi teacher in school, who was my first local guardian in Mumbai after I moved from Dehradun. Over the years, Apoorva has been the yellow brick road guarding my dreams.

She told me the first day she met me, 'You are going to be someone who will be heard. So you better work hard and hold on to your roots.'

Once, as I became a bit more engaged in acting during college, I received an offer to be part of a television reality show. I knew that the show was bad but the money was pretty good. When I called Apoorva for advice, she simply replied to my twenty-minute explanation with, 'The world is your playground. But you must be careful what shoes you play with.' I got the answer and declined the offer. Years later I realized I couldn't have made a better decision.

Victories will come. Failures will fizzle out. But to accommodate loud laughter after every dramatic sneeze, to order carrot cake and ginger shots in restaurants, to have someone's back will get you far ahead than you imagined. I am glad I have Apoorva on my team. I know now what grace and prayer together look like.

I am convinced that we all deserve people. Rainbow people. People who stand in the gap for you, let you talk silly and make mistakes. Pretty people. People who tell you Monday is a great day and that you are your own sunshine. Tamarind people. People who will never cease to surprise and dig astonishment out of you. Stardust people. Backbone people. Cherished hearts. Laugh out loud. Let's celebrate. People. If there is anything more that is needed, it's the opportunities to tell those people how important they are. All those people wrapped up in one person qualify to be a witness to the movie of your life. Someone who is a safety pin, a button, a bridge holding things together. Fixing the fail, connecting the ends. Always.

Think for a moment: Who would be ultra-perfect to understand the graphs of your life?

## 6

If you could only
see or hear for
the rest of your
life, which
sense would
you pick?

On a humid, rushed evening in Chennai, as we chatted on our way to the airport in the back seat of a stinky cab, Kari Seeley asked me this question. Kari and I had met at an arts fellowship exchange programme. The reason I remember everything about this day so clearly is because it was a difficult question. Maybe not for Kari because she works with people with special needs back home in Australia. (Although I, too, in the formative years of my career, worked with some incredible humans with special needs.) But the reason I was a bit dumbstruck with the question was because I approached it from a luxury standpoint rather than thought about it in terms of a disadvantage.

While I know most people would consider losing any of their senses a big tragedy, I actually had the honour to hear another point of view on this topic that never quite left me.

I must have been nineteen years old, travelling with an organization that worked with kids with special needs across the country. The prime focus for the initial months was visually impaired children. Workshop after workshop, I would gather insights, learnings and unforgettable memories from the students. I remember on one particular morning, the NGO's founder and I flew to Chennai to conduct a session in a hotel. There were about sixty-odd children who were either born blind or had lost their sight in an accident.

After a few hours of the usual warm-up games, theatre exercises and sharing of life lessons, I turned to the teacher of the group, a woman who was born blind. I asked her politely, 'Ever since I have been teaching and working with visually impaired children, I have seen that everyone around them builds a sympathy wall. Everyone is extra cautious about cracking jokes, behaving normally or talking like they usually talk. And this definitely arises out of the perception that the person in front of them is either inferior or severely disadvantaged, and if they don't behave seriously, they'll be labelled as insensitive.'

I told her that I had heard enough reasons why not being able to see was such a sad thing, but I was keen to explore if a student in the class believed there was an advantage to it as well. The teacher dismissed my idea with the casual remark, 'There is none.' She added, 'I am blind and I can tell you there is nothing good in the world about it.' This was disheartening, but I was determined to hear it from the students, because no matter how strong, it was ultimately her own subjective view.

So I pleaded and tried to convince her throughout the remaining session. At last, she told me, 'You can ask only five students. But in case any one of them fumbles or gets upset, you will have to abort the exercise and apologize.' I agreed.

I started with the first student, who heard the question and grinned widely, saying, 'Well, you can hear better. All your focus is on the sound and not the sight.' We all chuckled with him and clapped. The timid girl next to him stood as calmly as a monk. In defiance, her two ponytails moved fiercely with even a small movement of her head. I served her the question, 'What do you think is the benefit of being blind?' She thought for a moment, nodded her head like a seasoned philosopher and said, projecting her voice across the room, 'I can see a rainbow when there isn't one.'

She was eleven years old. And to tell you the truth, hearing those words, I felt as if she could see me. I felt a gaze through her latched eyelids arresting my attention. I did not know how to respond to her. I froze. Her answer was as bright and magical and meaningful as the rainbow she had claimed to see.

I saw the universe bowing down to her power of imagination. Ever since, whenever the serendipitous joy of witnessing a rainbow greets me, I recall that young girl in my classroom.

Kari looked at me, waiting for the answer to the question, 'If you could only see or hear for the rest of your life, which sense would you pick?' She added, 'I can do without seeing, but I love music too much to not be able to hear; that would be sad.'

I gave her an acknowledging smile.

You can guess my answer.

## 7

If you could ask
for one return
gift for all that
you have done
for the world,
what would
you ask
for?

The strange thing about earning your own money is that people stop buying you things. It is understandable for the big expenses one incurs that nobody but you should pay for. But I am referring to the less expensive things called 'gifts'. Things that have a high emotional price rather than material value.

My acting and teaching careers began at the start of my college life. The teaching career, though, generated no income, but the acting career increasingly did. I was paid a comfortable sum for my services on a television show. I could afford to buy most of the things I wanted. But, as the power to do that grew strong, I realized everyone around me stopped asking if I wanted anything or giving me gifts, assuming that I could buy whatever I desired.

The feeling of not being thought of in a random bazaar corner, a bookstore or at a street-side pop-up by family and friends was supremely discomforting. The purpose of gifts, I believe, is to invoke in the giver a conscious sense of acknowledgment for whom it's being bought, and in the receiver a profound fulfilment of being cared for. I was brushing my twinge of sadness under my own soppy pursuits until a very close hostel friend of mine, Avijit Pathak, came over to my room one evening and handed me a DVD. It read,

'The Best of Dolly Parton Songs'. At the time, I was absorbed in the melodies and music of Dolly Parton. Her songs would often play on loop on my computer. The fact that Avijit had noticed that pattern and got me something that would cheer me up brought back one of the greatest longings of the human heart: being remembered. He told me that on his way back from college, he saw a local vendor selling music cassettes and DVDs, and as soon as he saw Dolly Parton's name on one, he knew he had to buy it. He knew it would make my heart sing.

It very well did. Not only my heart but my eyes too. I cried and cried and cried for hours. An overwhelming feeling of care and comfort flooded my mind. I had nearly forgotten what it felt like to be gifted something without asking for it.

Over the years, I have become a bit more shameless in asking those I love for presents. In fact, I once made a list of the best gifts anyone could offer me. My list might spark in you an inspiration to create your own. It's a little poetic because I am a poet.

Gift me an anchor. So that it can remind me on days I feel inadequate that small hands can be capable of holding big ships on the shores of possibility.

Gift me some pickle in a jar. So that every time I dig in and pull out a piece to take a small bite, I can be aware that some things taste better with time. That good produce mixed with great effort, soaked in the sun of hope, can be preserved to savour with great delight at odd hours.

Gift me a long walk with you. And listen attentively. So that I can unburden the weight of each thought with every movement of my body. Letting my breath find a rhythm with my steps and my scattered mind.

Gift me a handwritten letter that smells of words you have woven to express yourself. To help me understand better anecdotes that I haven't lived yet. So that I can swing between your cursive sentences and dance unhinged between paragraphs and sentences. It will vouch that I was thought about from the start to the finish of a whole page.

Gift me soap bubbles. Bringing me to the sweet spot, waking me up to the realization that everything is in my control, yet everything goes in its own flow. So that I can create rainbows out of soap water and delightfully cheer for the simple joys of life. And be fully present in the process of enjoying each bubble before it bursts and dissolves into thin air.

Gift me a translated book of poetry in a language I do not speak. So that at each metaphor I can admire the talent of the poet who wrote something profound in the first place, added to that the translator who trekked through one language to climb the peaks of another. Through the caves of cultural contexts, cliffs of perspectives, two people who have amalgamated in a book, to help me lighten up on a laid-back Saturday night or at lunch on a chaotic Wednesday afternoon.

Gift me emotions morphed into tangible items, veiled by a feeling, guided by intention and offered with the universe as the witness to your deep and genuine kindness.

The simple act of gifting is layered with compassion, love, understanding, admiration, hope and attention, among other things. To receive a gift is to be apprised with the fact that you matter, that you belong and that you have not been forgotten or taken for granted. That someone actually, even if for a fleeting moment, paused to put your likes and dislikes on their priority list and made a conscious decision to share that with you. Gifting is an act of courage and meaningful connection for the giver; and an evident acceptance of value and gratitude for the receiver.

Gift people something that feels like a long, warm hug or conversations on laid-back chairs on Sunday afternoons, like alarm clocks that alert them to their potential, or something that screams you are here to stay, for whenever they need you, and that you care.

I know it might be awkward for most of us to straight up ask for gifts, but giving subtle hints to those we love is not a crime. If they don't get it, buy them something to make it obvious.

While writing this, the Dolly Parton song 'Coat of Many Colours' popped up in my playlist. I am now wondering who could gift me that. My coat of many colours.

## 8

What makes
life worth
living for
you?

If there was one thing I could change when I hear someone say: 'I hope you find your calling', I would gently tweak it to: 'I hope you find the direction of your calling'.

What you dedicate your life to is the direction of your calling, or what you hope your calling is. That is the only thing you can do. Because the calling evolves over time. It doesn't rest as one objective, but manifests into many different forms. I am a bit wary of people who make finding their calling sound like discovering a pot of gold at the end of the rainbow or stumbling upon an oil well in their backyard. Perhaps this is why so many people, after realizing their so-called 'calling', hesitate to grow out of it to do better things. They guard themselves amid the perception of their purpose, whereas the purpose itself is an emotion in constant evolution.

Your calling, I have come to believe, morphs into ideas, projects, ambitions, strategies and dreams you never even fathomed in your creative mind. You have to do a decade's worth of homework to even begin conceiving them.

When I started collecting life lessons at fourteen, I did not aspire to start a global organization with so many creative projects across the spectrum. What I really hoped would happen was that, with all the wisdom of the world in my journals, by the time I was eighteen, I would be the first person in human history to commit no mistakes. I swear I thought that.

But as I turned seventeen and inched towards my eighteenth birthday, I started realizing it was impossible to not make any mistakes. In fact, on the contrary, *that* would be a far bigger mistake. Collecting life lessons from people who belonged to all walks of life revealed to me that I had the choice and power to not commit the same mistake that a million people had already made, and could share what happened at the end of that newer experience. It was like going to watch a movie knowing how it ended. Therefore, I was liberated into pushing the limits in each aspect of my life: work, relationship, friendship, among others.

In the process of executing a project, the moment an outcome or learning would become predictable, I would alter the plotline a little to arrive at new discoveries. When I look back to take stock of the kind of work I have done, I think this shift in perspective has been the major catalyst.

Otherwise, there is no solid reason for a young boy with no big connections or family wealth being able to spend ninety days in Europe, documenting the learnings of refugees displaced by the conflict in Syria, or collect stories from a remote village and depict them through paintings on walls.

In 2017, alarmed by the migration in the hills, we adopted a charming 600-year-old abandoned ghost village in the mountains of Uttarakhand, India, named Saur. Out of the 200 families that once lived there, only twelve remained. I was determined to trace and document the life lesson of each family that belonged to Saur. And although up until then I had predominantly used the tool of education to pass on wisdom, I realized, being amid the villagers, that it would not be sufficient to just collect and write down their learnings. Given the deserted and uninhabited houses, it was imperative to make them more colourful for the last remaining twelve families. This is how the component of painting their folktales, cultural anecdotes, rural wisdom and age-old philosophies, along with the life lessons, came into being. My dear friend and celebrated muralist Poornima Sukumar spearheaded the project and helped see my dream light of the day.

I used to tell everyone, 'I know that of all the things I could attempt, I won't be a director for sure.' But life knows all the tricks to make you accept that you should never say never! When the video footage of the project came in, I had to stitch a narrative out of it because I had conceived it in the first place and was witness to each element of its making. So, I donned the hat of a director, first reluctantly then more naturally and eventually more enthusiastically. The thing that kept me from feeling excited from the very beginning was the conditioning of the 'calling' I mentioned at the beginning of this chapter. Based on what I thought the definition of a director was and my claim to my friends that I wasn't ever going to be one, I hesitated initially to hold the rope and set sail.

Of course, the experience taught me that I could be one because I was a storyteller. And that role and its form could expand into a lot more mediums if I was open to it.

It takes great courage to play many different roles in one single life. To experience all the things you love or live or savour or serve, and not be ashamed of it. The fact is, we are going to die. And if we have already signed up for that adventure, the most unknown of all, should anything else scare us at all? That driving class we have been meaning to take, the ballet we wish to perform, the cooking, the singing, the off-roading, skydiving?

People can only make you feel bad about being a jack of all trades when you deny you are one. When you announce you want to be a jack, the world gives up on making you the master of one.

Author Maya Angelou wrote, 'When you know better, you do better.' I do know better now, and, consequently, I want to be many things: maps that guide people home, prayers that help faith survive, a lullaby that hums people to a peaceful sleep, and most of all, a river that travels far and beyond and nourishes everything it passes.

I don't know what makes life worth living for you, but I do know that lifting the pressure of finding your calling might contribute to its value. Don't allow yourself to be cushioned by your ability to trust and to solve matters of mistrust. You will be reminded to trust your intuition and to set an intention while you do so. Perhaps, every once in a while, switch tracks, set the volume to an unassuming level. While you blindfold your courage with the strap of clarity, try not to easily embrace the purpose that longs for home, but rather challenge the intention that seeks your help in finding an existence. In the process, your calling might evolve.

## 9

If you had three
seconds of courage
to share something
you haven't
necessarily before,
what would
you share?

I would share that I wasn't always sure or comfortable with talking about my favourite life lessons in front of the camera. All my friends will tell you otherwise. I have been talking as comfortably as breathing for all my school, college and work life. But contrary to the popular belief, I kept pushing the idea of filming a whole series of myself sitting in front of a lens, dispensing heart-warming learnings. I can admit now, I was considerably confident of the lessons, but somewhere sceptical of people's opinion of the narrator; that is, me.

Then something happened and that fear evaporated into thin air.

Last year, as I queued up for an airport security check, I noticed a well-dressed, tall and sharp man in his late fifties collapse all of a sudden. He was reading a magazine one minute and the next he was on the floor, vulnerable and still. That incident left quite an impression on my conscious memory. As people and the airport staff rushed to check on him, to give him CPR, I froze in shock. I did not know the man, but I was overwhelmed, thinking about the overall uncertainty of life. I wondered about the things that were still on his to-do list, people he would have wanted to call that afternoon or things that he had postponed doing all his life.

I had been quite social about sharing my ideas and stories, but that incident pushed me a little harder to pass on whatever I had been given with others as soon as I could.

After years of contemplation, overthinking, procrastination and request messages from people, I finally summoned the courage to launch the digital series *Twice as Wise*. Through this, I share some of the most memorable, soul-stirring and easy-to-imbibe life lessons we have documented. Each episode is centred on a life lesson I received at Project FUEL, one that has created an immense impact on the lives of others. Each episode is about five minutes long and has the story behind the life lesson, how I designed it and passed it on. And finally, it talks about how the person watching the video can interpret and internalize that life lesson. My narrative is intercut with footage from FUEL workshops and my travels over the years.

The most beautiful part about this series is the authentic human wisdom that comes not from masters and mentors of popular culture, but from common people in common corridors of life from all around the world.

And after two seasons of the show, I can tell you that it has expanded the bandwidth of my on-the-ground classroom— from an online platform to a larger global audience. It feels like the right thing to do. In fact, it's my pilgrimage now.

The reward of courage has been multifold. Compliments from strangers at airports, love notes in my Instagram DMs and countless Facebook messages. All this strings together my strength, message after message after message. The most magnified validation came last December, just a day before I commenced the shoot for the second season of *Twice as Wise*.

I am sharing the letter with the due permission of the sender, in the hope that it will encourage you to take charge of whatever it is that is bothering you. A girl who watched the first season of *Twice as Wise* wrote:

Hi Deepak,

You have made such a huge impact on my life. I would not be the person I am today without you and I know that you will keep inspiring me to become an even better version of myself. You taught me the wonders of people and how they can change my life. A year ago, I was diagnosed with schizophrenia after I was raped by a stranger. Schizophrenia is a mental disorder that is usually characterized by delusions, hallucinations, and other cognitive difficulties. It is a lifelong struggle. I see his face daily and I feel he is following me. I wasn't able to go out of my house for days and days. I would lock myself out, shout out loud, cry and even hurt myself. I could see his face daily and sometimes he used to talk with me, triggering a huge wave of negativity within me. I was so scared that I won't be able to survive this fight. Medication or even therapy wasn't working well because I didn't have internal motivation. I was helpless inside my own den. I didn't talk much, didn't do anything and even forgot to trust my own friends, family. It was a very low point in my life. I didn't know how to pick up the pieces.

Just say that it was a beautiful day, my friend came to visit me and she forced me to go on my social media and be a bit active there, that's when I bumped into your video series 'TWICE AS WISE' on Facebook. Trust me! You flattered me there. It was just the kick I needed to bring myself back and start that battle within me. I was so moved by it. That was the first time I cried and cried because I was feeling worthy of myself. I touched a human for the first time after that incident. I hugged my dear friend and cried to her. That moment was the best one. My friend had goose bumps all over seeing me. That was the biggest progress I made in days. I decided to never let myself down again. I picked myself up. I was done dealing with my rapist's bullshit. I was done with the voices inside me. I made a routine to see your videos daily and visit your 'PROJECT FUEL' page in order to keep myself motivated. I took great care of myself. Slowly, I show really great progress. I am still not cured fully. It's going to stay forever within me. I still hear him say negative things about me, I still hear his footsteps following me but hey! You know what my life is amazing now because I can answer them all back. I can just let it go in ignorance.

Nowadays, I don't look back when I hear footsteps behind me, I keep moving ahead. You have taught me that you don't always have to be strong. You are allowed to break down as long as you pick yourself back up and keep moving forward. I am a fighter and I will always be. Thanks for making those videos and all the other amazing content you create through people. Thanks for being a ray of sunshine and hope in my life. Above all, thanks for saving a life like me. You are valued and mean a lot to me. 'If I won't tell my story, no one else will ever tell it' so here I am, sending you lots of hugs, warmth and affection.

I am moved to tears just rereading it here. I believe we all experience moments when we are shaken to our core, even damaged in one form or another. The point to observe is that while some people immediately start with the process of inner healing all by themselves, others wait an entire lifetime for someone else to fix them.

As my dearest friend Tapshi Dhanda aptly puts it, 'Don't be in denial. It doesn't solve anything.' I had to stop denying that I could speak well in front of the camera, could script anecdotes into powerful narratives, and could make a connection several thousand miles away from people through a screen.

No wonder my biggest learning in 2016 was: 'Your talent is not your gift, it is your responsibility.' Ever since I saw that man collapse at the airport, I am trying to live with an awareness of my responsibility and to offer what I do know for sure. The joy of sharing an idea, passing on a learning, handing out goodness is always rooted in gratitude but to experience it one must show courage unfailingly.

## 10

Are
you
okay?

These three words form the easiest question to ask, but the most difficult to answer. I am quite sure you are asked this question at least thirty times in a week on average.

But it takes temerity to answer truthfully. Most people respond automatically with, 'Fine. Thank you. And you?' There are very few people I have met in my life who share exactly how they feel in that moment. One of them was the actor Abhay Deol. I remember visiting his house with a common friend. He graciously welcomed us inside. As we entered, I asked the obvious courteous question, 'So how are you?' And he immediately responded, 'Well, today a bit irritated with something. But I hope it gets better as the day moves forward.' I was amazed at his honesty and refreshed too.

I have always used the 'How are you/Are you okay?' question as a filter for people in my life. Whenever someone asks me the same, I purposely try to be as truthful, descriptive and expatiated as possible, just to gauge if the person really cares to know how I am feeling or is asking just as a formality. Some people look perplexed with my long answers, some are distracted, some interrupt to move on, and a select few listen intently. I see a pattern there; they all end up becoming people I like to meet for more than just work conversations.

Many of them, over time, have become very close friends of mine.

I hope your answer to the question is a resounding yes! But if it's a 'no', that's all right too. You don't have to feel the pressure to conform and answer in the affirmative because it is a popular thing to do. I consider 'Are you okay?' a critical question to ask yourself every now and then. It will allow you to pause and reflect and take notice of your situation. Your emotions will start to surface because you are paying attention to what you are undergoing. In all cases, whether you are doing great, just all right or not so good, you have the opportunity to do something about it. The good feeling can be magnified to recognize what you are grateful for, and it must be sustained, the 'okay-okay' situation will help you comprehend if you are holding back your reactions or are genuinely not affected, and the 'not so good' one will allow you to not be in denial but rather take action, even if it's just to accept you are not feeling all right.

My only suggestion in times like these would be to guide yourself out of situations that are toxic. To sulk is convenient and endlessly consuming. It's easy to blame and to think the world is conspiring against you. Easier than putting on a smile despite the hurt. Gather your scattered pain and make sense of it. Start small. Look for your favourite song on the radio. Mix two of your favourite flavours of ice cream together. Be in bed longer, hugging the pillow, but without any self-loathing. Smile at strangers. Take time to heal, but with hope, not disappointment. Being happy is a full-time job, and you can choose to be employed with a little help.

One can know a lot about people with just two simple questions: 'Who are you?' and 'How are you?' I hope that whenever you get to ask that, you are able to see the truest side of another person, and whenever you get the chance to answer it, you are able to speak your truth—loud and clear.

## 11

Are you grateful
to your pain
that it chose
you over
everyone
else?

Healing is a confusing and complex process. It doesn't look like the swish of a magic wand as soon as the words 'I forgive you' are said. It often seems like it's been resolved in the moment and then suddenly resurfaces, unannounced, as your emotional balance churns to spit out doubt, loneliness and self-hate. Healing doesn't dissolve, dispel or damage pain; it allows everything around it to become more immune and loving. Healing allows you to live and breathe, over and over, when the storms seem too tough to battle out.

I read somewhere online, 'It eventually gets better; without any sort of explanation you just wake up one morning and you are not as upset any more.' This is what healing feels like, I guess. The day you don't need any justification, any amount of convincing, any need to retell old stories. But it takes a while to get there. Some days you run, others you crawl, and on most you work towards being okay.

I am trying to be grateful to my pain, that it chose me because somewhere it knew I could handle it well and eventually heal. We all have been hit by trust storms, shaken by doubt about those we cared for deeply. Our fragile hearts have been troubled by judgement, our windpipes choked with remarks that question our affection. A cyclone of meltdowns and a hurricane of hurt. But despite the repercussions, the displacement and the chaos, we are still here, waiting for the sun to hold the sky in hope, the moon to sing a lullaby to bruised dreams, and tracing a way back to whatever was our idea of love, of loving and being loved in the first place.

I know that for most people, the pain emerges out of a romantic setback. We are capable of dealing with career, financial or material losses, but in matters of the heart, we have to build a muscle or pull ourselves towards the altar of self-care and gratitude. Oh! It is hard. Maybe the hardest. But you have to let go. Let go to the point where their name doesn't bother you. The sight of them getting praised by someone doesn't flick your mood off. You have to embrace the letting go to a place where you can weave them in conversations consciously and yet remain graceful. Of course that is going to be hard, but that's how you let go. Dumbo!

While answering this question once, I wrote a small poem of encouragement for myself. I offer it to you:

You gave love your trust.
You gave pain your judgement.
When love showed up, the arc of your lips rose
For pain you raised only your eyebrows
You gave love every friend you earned
To pain you shut down access to even yourself
You offer love multiple chances
You served pain with no time whatsoever.
You gave love your whole being
And to pain never an opportunity to win you back,
You know what?
Let the pain stay for a while because the love could not.
It's all right.

## 12

If forgiveness
was essential to
breathing, how
often would
you choke?

I had read about this guesthouse in Varanasi, India, where people check in to die. It's called 'Kashi Labh Mukti Bhawan'. There is a strong belief among many Hindus that if you breathe your last in Kashi (Varanasi), you attain what is popularly known as 'Kashi Labh' or 'the fruit of Kashi'—moksha. Now, the interesting part is that you are allowed only two weeks stay to die. If you are still around after two weeks, you will have to check out. So, you really have to be sure.

I was curious to know what those people had learnt in their lives who had not only accepted death as a reality but were also anticipating it with a timer. So I went there. Other than the people who came there to die, the most fascinating personality was Bhairav Nath Shukla, the manager of Mukti Bhawan for forty-four years. He had witnessed more than 12,000 deaths. I asked him what he had learnt after experiencing both life and death at such close quarters. He shared with me twelve life lessons from his long-standing career.

One of the most resonating life lessons was, 'Resolve all conflicts before you go.'

He told me the story of Shri Ram Sagar Mishr, a Sanskrit scholar of his times. Mishr was the eldest of six brothers and was closest to the youngest one. Years ago, an ugly argument between the two brothers had led to a wall being built to partition the house.

In his final days, Mishr walked to the guesthouse, carrying his little paan case, and asked for room number 3 to be reserved for him. He was sure he would pass away on the sixteenth day after his arrival. On the fourteenth day, he said, 'Ask my estranged brother of forty years to come see me. This bitterness makes my heart heavy. I am anxious to resolve every conflict.'

A letter was sent out. On the sixteenth day, when the youngest brother arrived, Mishr held his hand and asked him to bring down the wall dividing the house. He asked his brother for forgiveness. Both brothers wept, and mid-sentence, Mishr stopped breathing. His face became calm. He was gone in a moment.

That anecdote seems straight out of a folk fiction book, but Shukla has seen this story play out in many forms over the years. He said, 'People carry so much baggage unnecessarily all through their lives, only wanting to drop it at the very end of their journey. The trick doesn't lie in not having conflicts but in resolving them as soon as one can.' At the end of each day, do not go to bed without resolving each argument, doubt and resentment you might be holding. After all, the good news is you are alive. The bad news is no one knows for how long.

## 13

How can someone
make you feel
more loved?

I remember exactly where and when that question was born. At a summit in Shimla, after my talk at an event, I was approached by an inquisitive yet shy college student, Vishnu Kaushal, to give him some time. Earlier, I would just readily say yes and sit for hours, paying attention to every word the person across me had to offer. But over time, I realized I enjoyed going for walks and discussing life with total strangers, rather than plopping myself on a couch and shifting uncomfortably to find the right posture and the will to offer my unshakeable attention.

The other thing I practise now with people who admire my work and wish to speak to me is play fair and ask them questions too. I am unabashedly open in admitting that I haven't figured it all out. We are in this journey together, some definitely further along than others in some departments, so why not harness the collective wisdom? So, I usually make a pact—if you wish to ask me questions then I will ask you some as well. We go for a walk and unfurl as many answers as we can.

The boy, Vishnu, went first, asking me about my inspirations and whether I felt lonely sometimes. I took my turn and asked him to share something he hadn't necessarily revealed before. Our conversation choreographed its way through questions and answers, both honest and heartfelt. As we neared the end of our long walk to head back to the summit, it was his turn to ask me the final question. I still remember we paused on a red-tiled floor, the sky a shade of violet, blue and raspberry red, faded music playing in a rusty Maggi shop nearby. His face was calm and curious and he asked me a question I had never been asked before: 'If "What is your life lesson?" was already taken as a question, what question would you ask the world as often?'

I'll tell you my answer in a while, but let me first share the physical reaction that question evoked in me. I felt giddy, a fleet of tiny hair rose on my arms, I felt a certain loss of existence, and I had to breathe deeply to ensure oxygen was still flowing through my lungs. Quite a dramatic reaction to a simple question, one would think. But, to be honest, I had never ever, even in my wildest dreams, considered the alternative to 'What is your life lesson?' I had been asking this question since I was fourteen years old. My entire career was shaped on the innocence and strength of its foundation. In the instance he asked me the question, I felt almost threatened with a kind of nakedness, as if someone had pulled my blanket away and exposed me.

Despite this towering emotion, I loved the question. It was carefully considered, personal yet poignant. I thought for a while, stripping off the accolades, ideas and intentions of the previous question. I summoned the courage to draft a new one, 'How can someone make you feel more loved?' As I uttered those words, an adrenaline rush took over my system. The pores on my face opened, my back straightened a bit, and my eyes had a new shine. I felt energized with what I believed could be my new question. And I meant it. I could start my journey all over again with this new question if I had to.

More recently, while asking a close friend 'How can someone make you feel more loved?' I was demanded to answer it as well. Here's what I shared:

'Someone can make me feel more loved by accepting the love I have to offer them without any insecurity or cynicism. To genuinely absorb the juicy broth of care that I have in my bones. If someone can do that, what an honour it is to love.'

Over the last few months, I have asked many people this question, and many people have responded saying, 'You can make me feel loved by listening to me.' There is an innate need in all of us to be heard. To be recognized for who we are. And hopefully accepted as we are.

The interesting thing to attempt is to make people fall in love with themselves a bit more. In a world of social media evaluation, constant comparisons, false perceptions and derogatory comments, the easiest thing to do is to make someone feel lost, less valued, like they don't belong and they don't matter. The harder thing to push for is to make the same person, who has been brainwashed by the standards of pretentious beauty and unauthentic power, believe that they are beautiful. And that if they feel it for a brief moment, they are quite further along to actually living it routinely. It takes years for a river to originate and a lifetime to navigate through the face of the earth, nourishing civilizations. And for us, a few seconds coupled with ignorance to pollute it. People are like rivers. Don't dump the garbage of your hate into their sacred waters. Rather, ask them and yourself, 'How can someone make you feel more loved?'

## 14

How do you want people to discover you long after you are gone?

'How do you want people to discover you long after you are gone?' This question popped up in my head as an answer to a question that was emailed by someone.

The person wrote, 'Deepak, I want to serve the world like you. But how do I find my purpose?' Despite the fact that there are several suggestions available—like quotes by Elizabeth Gilbert, 'Follow your curiosity and not your passion', and Kurt Vonnegut, 'What should young people do with their lives today? Many things, obviously. But the most daring thing is to create stable communities in which the terrible disease of loneliness can be cured'—there are some who still feel confused and clueless.

I have realized that no matter what the answer is, the question does put some pressure on us to find our calling. But what can ease the palpitations of the heart on hearing that question is a rephrased version of it. I try to break the magnitude of my purpose into how I would like to be discovered. Note that I don't use the word 'remembered' here. I think there is a certain wave of expectations about how you would like to be recalled and rejoiced over after you are dead. I cautiously use the word 'discovered', because there is room for serendipity in it. A fleeting moment of possibility that someone may or may not come across you even after you have transitioned from your physical form.

I love that anecdote about the Mexican traditional belief that people die three deaths. The first death is when our bodies cease to function—when our hearts no longer beat of their own accord, when our gaze no longer has depth or weight, when the space we occupy slowly loses its meaning. The second death comes when the body is lowered into the ground, returned to Mother Earth, out of sight. The third death, the most definitive death, is when there is no one left alive to remember us.

Knowing that you will die, and more so, accepting its inevitability, encourages you to take a moment to think about how you want people to discover you. It may allow you to look beyond the popular buzz of career and other conventional callings! If you want people to discover you in random people's conversations, you should go out and speak with more strangers. If you want people to come across you through art, you should definitely dedicate time to creating more art. And so on.

My quest to learn from striking experiences has taken me to the holy city of Varanasi many times. During my first visit, in a matter of ten minutes, I witnessed seven dead bodies being brought to the cremation shore of Manikarnika Ghat, as six others burnt on pyres that were already there. The tea seller–guide friend I had made on the ghat summarized everything I felt about this experience. With three funeral pyres in the backdrop, he said with a straight face, 'So many people have given up their lives to make those who are alive understand what really matters. But they don't get it until they themselves have to sacrifice their lives to make someone else understand all over again.'

Now, my heart rejoices to imagine that some day, someone will discover me through the route of life lessons, and maybe in that revelatory moment they will try to think of what they have learnt in their own life. Ah! So much joy!

## 15

What do you
not have that
you really,
really want?

I'm not lured by speedy cars. I don't fancy exotic video games, duty-free perfumes, branded shoes. Not even watches for that matter.

I don't have anything against people who care for those things. I am happy for them, but when I take my own case into consideration, I feel delight, bordering on relief, that my aspirations are not rooted in the purchase of price-tag-heavy things. It is a blessing, perhaps, given the work I do. I can focus my energy on supporting the communities I have to build and setting up an office that I have to make as comfortable as a monastery so that it can house every creative friend I have and the people who inspire me.

I can count on my fingers the four most expensive things I have bought for myself so far in life. The first item was a pair of Levi's jeans in Mumbai. I had just arrived in the glittery city for college, having left my humble town of Dehradun. It wasn't that I had never worn jeans before, but that I had never spent almost 2000 rupees on buying one pair. Growing up in a middle-class family, that was the total amount my parents would spend to buy clothes for themselves, my sister and I. And they would still have money left to pick up a dress or trousers for a cousin we met at a family wedding. I remember standing at the mall in Mumbai and calling my parents seven times, asking permission to buy those jeans. They were incredibly generous. So I did pick it up. It fit so well. I wore it for many years after that day, and every time I did, I felt like royalty.

The second item was a Nike jacket for 5000 rupees. I saw it in a store in Pune. My friend Aprajita almost became half a lawyer convincing me to buy it. But it took me nearly six months of convincing myself to take the plunge. I still have it. It is reversible. The woollen side has faded out, but the slippery, shiny latex side is as good as brand new. It comes handy for all my projects in the mountains, a shield against the biting cold on freezing snowy nights.

The third was an iPhone, the cost of which made my parents think I could buy a small piece of land if I added some more money, instead of a tabular metal device on my hand. But it was convenient and I needed it, given how many times my old phone had hung right before an important meeting. Once, it took an hour to reboot just before I started reciting lyrics to a director at a music studio. I did not lose the film, thankfully, but did part ways with the phone.

The fourth was an original Fjallraven Kanken bag from Sweden, which I bought on one of my trips there. I had seen the smartly designed, thin-strapped, sleek bag hanging from the shoulders of many Europeans through my travels. I had been eyeing it since then. Finally, in 2017, I validated my decision of going to a store in Malmo, Sweden, and gifting myself an original one with the simple assertion that I deserved it. What I truly love is how this small bag that is just the length of my forearm can fit a universe inside it. I shall continue to test its holding capacity as long as I have it intact.

That's it. Other than these four times, I cannot recall having an aching urge to buy anything for myself. I love gifting things to other people, though. Not huge and expensive gifts, but small and thoughtful items of personal use.

I don't judge or criticize people who wear expensive brands or buy handbags that cost five-digit figures because it is a gift to be able to do so. To some people, clothes and jewellery are art, and they like to be collectors.

I would like to try it some day. To be rich and comfortable enough to walk into a showroom and pick a suit without looking at the price tag. Until then, I am grateful to derive my sense of value from the geraniums blooming on the sidewalk, the new carpet in the bedroom, the water holder I have been planning to buy for a long time (I can almost imagine it at the office front door), and, most of all, the books I am planning to order from Amazon this weekend.

Whatever it is, just ensure that your sense of peace doesn't get hammered by the desire for the thing. That Nike jacket posed a serious threat in this regard. There will always be something we really want. But what are our resources? How much satisfaction will it bring? Is it only costing us money or much more? These are some of the questions we should ask before swiping a card.

## 16

# What saved you?

I remember telling my classmates at my college graduation, 'Your hope is your knowledge.' As I grow into more and more adulthood, I realize a fuller meaning of that statement. As a young child who was bullied constantly through school, complete with all the name-calling, shaming and backbiting, I wonder how I survived. One of the strongest reasons I land upon is that I was hopeful of a better future. I was assured, I don't know at that time by what, that there would be a point in time when my voice would matter, my words would count and I would be heard for what I had to say. I had to consistently and repeatedly tell myself a positive narrative about what was going to happen to me. Something controlled by me and not those who considered me weak. My hope really was my knowledge. And I used it to align myself to things I liked doing most—poetry, debating, writing, acting, studying, all of it. Even today, when I look out at the expanse of times to come, I know my hope is guiding me to a beautiful world I am helping build.

I find those who say they are not hopeful hypocritical, because it is impossible for us to be alive without hope. The world feeds upon the hope of so many people.

A farmer ploughs his land, sows the seed and does everything in his might, but at the end hopes for the rain to arrive on time and in just the right proportion to nurture his crops. That hope makes its way to your plate every day. The fisherman who battles with the sea in order to catch fresh fish would not risk it if he did not believe in the possibility of catching some every time he swings his fishnet into the charged waters. The same is true for the coders of our mobile apps, the pilots of our airplanes, the teachers in our schools, and everyone who is moving the world forward in a routine manner, with extraordinary hope. Next time you call yourself hopeless, take into consideration all the hope that reaches you in every gesture, and acknowledge and appreciate it. Just because you can't see it yet does not mean it doesn't exist.

I see myself as an active ambassador of hope, because that was what helped me cope and care when I really did not have to oblige. It bolstered my confidence and allowed me to see the world with a sense of wonder.

The journey to your own empowerment after you have hit rock bottom, or to your revival after you have reached breaking point, seems a long and excruciating one. 'How do I begin', you ask?

Well, you begin by not being harsh on yourself. Then, you turn towards accepting yourself and not pushing away those who still guard over you. You begin by taking off the metrics, the numbers, the labels off your back. You turn a deaf ear to the name-calling. You avoid the itch to fire back, retaliate, prove a point or start a debate. You begin by turning up the volume against the voices in your own head. You begin by catching yourself as soon as you start overthinking. Or over-reacting. You begin by starting over. You begin with hope.

I did.

## 17

Which goodbye
will be the
hardest for
you to
say?

Of all the tough acts in life, saying a heartfelt goodbye is probably the hardest. No words quite gather themselves together to form a definitive sentence—one that can shape itself into a bowl and hold all the aching emotions of this heart. Maybe because to say goodbye is to acknowledge that the end is almost here. Perhaps it is coming to terms with the dawn of new beginnings, but only after engaging with the dusk of what had once existed. People transitioning into stories, morphing into bygone experiences, slipping into anecdotes about what once made up a full day, packed with twenty-four hours of being part of reality. And now, those very twenty-hour hours consist suddenly of nothing but capsules of nostalgia that will unexpectedly show up, asking for a home amidst conversations with strangers and moments of self-reflection.

I maintained a journal and wrote in it every day on my Africa tour, an act I consider heroic given my exceptional talent for procrastination; my mind has the ability to hold on to memories of things that happen, and the way I feel when they do, so I put off writing about them. Yet it took me by surprise, reading this little excerpt from one of the last pages of my journal.

I often wonder how I survived, saying goodbye to all the bright smiles in Nepal post the 2015 earthquake. I taught there for almost two weeks, and not a single day went by when I was not aware of the privilege we have to simply breathe. I have had marvellous opportunities to immerse myself in classrooms across the world—from middle-school students in Afghanistan to refugees from Syria; from sex workers in Kamathipura to people inhabiting the last village before a glacier. And each one of them offered to be a folk melody that one might forget the lyrics of, but every once in a while, one might find oneself humming its tune unassumingly. As an educator and a conversationalist, I have realized that I offer myself completely to people when I am with them. There is no hint of reservation, and full access to whatever knowledge I have and can share. The act I find challenging is when the class or the conversation is over, to pick yourself up from across someone and head towards the door. To lift your arms to give them a parting hug, when you don't exactly know the right words to tell them how you feel. Words are complex and diverse, and so, I return to what I wrote in the journal as an antidote, for my healing to begin.

> Goodbye is most certainly the toughest word in the dictionary. It is too much and too little. It is reckless and riveting. It makes everything intractable. But there is a trick to passing this exam as well, that is, filling your heart with gratitude and placing the words on your lips, saying 'Thank you' more often. And whispering in soft tones to yourself that 'it's okay'. It's okay, wanting to simply say, genuinely, with a hint of hope to people and places—'Goodbye'.

The goodbye I will perhaps have the hardest time acknowledging is the one to my sister, Deepika, the greatest gift I was given in this lifetime. I can't wait for those who tell me that I am gifted or special to meet my wonder sibling. In her simplicity, she is abundant. With her power to hold space for others, she beats the universe hands down. That is going to be a tough goodbye, I am sure.

## 18

What was taken
from you
but never
returned?

Your favourite dress? The remote-controlled car? Your personal diary? Books? How far back can you think? How deep you want to dive? Your guardian? A friend you believed you had almost for life? Your childhood? Its innocence? Your designation at work? A sense of security or self-respect?

It is unarguably true, yet undeniably hurtful, to accept that we all have handed out a piece of our puzzle that we can never get back. Something that constructed a part of us and made the collective seem meaningful. It is imperative to observe, however, how we have coped with that loss. If we have at all, that is. What value does its residual presence amount to now? Is it just a swallowed memory or bereavement we carry through? Does it reflect in our poetry? The colours we adorn? Has the mourning over the dispossession ended or does it now lust after a bigger audience?

When I was young, my tuition teacher, an old, wrinkled man, would tell us stories every day after class. There was nothing I yearned for more than those fables laced with moral wisdom; spilling out of this man who seemed to be from another planet where people were born as old as him. Or so thought my naive childhood brain.

There is a particular story he told us often that I recollect. A story about a crow and a peacock. The peacock, he said, was born beautiful head-to-toe. With its colourful tail feathers outstretched, it strutted about, dancing happily in the woods. One day, the crow had to attend a lavish wedding in a distant forest. It thought, 'I do not have the glowing skin of a parrot, the grace of a swan, the colour of a peacock or the charm of a sparrow.' It considered borrowing something significant from a friend to show up at the gala and make a memorable statement. Approaching his dear friend, the peacock, the crow asked if he could borrow its neat legs for the function. The peacock, out of genuine compassion, swapped its sharp, agile and gorgeous legs with the crow's rickety, wrinkly legs. The crow, embellished with this new look, visited the city. But when it got back, it refused to return the peacock its legs.

That is why they say, when it rains, peacocks dance in sheer joy until their eyes notice their feet. Tears stream down their faces, in anguish for the ravishing legs that the crow took but never returned.

## 19

What do
you most
believe in?

'In myself'—I think that is my answer.

A few weeks after I arrived in Mumbai from Dehradun, I headed to the office of CNN-IBN, one of the biggest news channels in India. When I reached, I requested to meet the senior bureau chief. I was made to wait for a few hours; rightly so, because I had come unannounced with no prior appointment.

I was brimming with an incredible amount of excitement to start my career as a journalist. I was convinced that I was fit for the job and they must hire me immediately. When I was ushered in to meet the man, I had a whole speech ready in my head. He started asking questions about my background, my qualifications and other details. I informed him that after my final school exams, I had worked at a local newspaper as a reporter and writer. 'That is great,' he replied. 'You are passionate, I can tell.'

'That means I can start work tomorrow?' I asked.

This made him almost burst into laughter. 'It doesn't work like that. You have to start by interning with us, and eventually, when you finish college, we can see if there is a position open for you.'

'Sure. So I'll join as an intern,' I replied, unaffected by this sharp cut on the fabric of my journalistic ambitions.

'How old are you, though, given you have just joined college?'

'I am seventeen.'

'Ah! We only take interns who are eighteen and above.'

'I'll be eighteen in four months.'

'Sure. Come back then.'

I couldn't argue with their company policy. So I left with a new desire to be eighteen soon enough. The man himself might not have thought much of that incident because he must be meeting many people like me on a weekly basis.

On 18 November 2009, I woke up early. It was my birthday, and time to tend to unfinished conversations. I rang up the bureau chief and told him, 'Do I join tomorrow then? I am eighteen and legally fit to intern with you.'

He laughed again over the phone and said, 'It's hard to forget you. Sure you can join. But for now, enjoy your birthday.'

The first few months on the job were hectic. Some reporters gave me stacks of tapes to ingest into the system, some made me transcribe what I call the history of the world, and others simply ignored me. Even then, I repeatedly made efforts to request for a field assignment. I knew I belonged outside, with a microphone in hand, asking people questions.

After two months of doing a desk job, one afternoon, I was told the Delhi sports team needed someone to interview a popular Sri Lankan cricketer who was in Mumbai to walk the ramp for a designer. He had recently been removed from the team for one-day matches. The sports team in Delhi wanted his reaction to being thrown out.

It turned out that just that afternoon, every reporter at the Mumbai office was already out covering a story. The other interns were also unavailable for the assignment. They were left with no option but to send me.

Armed with a cameraman, I arrived at the lobby of a swanky five-star hotel. The pressure of this being my first field assignment propelled me to reach much before time. We logged our details at the press desk.

Right before the cricketer arrived, the publicist announced, 'This is a fashion show, therefore no cricket questions should be asked. Every channel will be allowed to ask only two questions.' This clearly indicated that the answers we all had hoped for weren't going to be handed out. The publicist added, 'And we will follow a sequence.' Meaning the channel that arrived first would have the first interview.

I looked at the questionnaire that the Delhi sports team had sent. It was full of questions about cricket and harsh observations like, 'How does it feel to be replaced by younger players?' I looked up and the cricketer was in front of me. It was my turn to ask him questions.

In my nervousness, I asked him something related to fashion, something very fatuous. Two questions later, I was shoved back and another news reporter took over.

Although my work was over, I felt a strong urge to not give up. My mind raced, thinking that this was my first job. I would be labelled as someone who couldn't get a story out. I did not want that shame. Not because I wanted to be popular, but because I believed I could do better. I could ask this cricketer why he wasn't selected without offending him.

I waited until the last few channels finished their interviews. I walked up to the publicist and told her that I was the first channel to do an interview, but I couldn't get my questions answered well, and there was some technical glitch in the recording. She agreed to give me a second chance but told me to wait.

In the meantime, I took all the hard questions and turned them into soft, conversational concerns. When my turn came, I asked the cricketer, 'As fans, we miss seeing you on the ground doing what you do best. Is there a specific consolation response you can give us while we watch the upcoming one-day series?' 'You have been a senior player. How do you see the young players taking forward your legacy?' I asked every question on the sheet. But in my own style.

We were the only channel that had a response from the cricketer on not playing in the series. That ensured there would be no more dreary work of transcribing tapes for me. I started being sent out more because my interviewing skills were appreciated.

But the way I look at it is that my unshakeable belief in myself got me into that room with the bureau chief, encouraged me to call him as soon as I turned eighteen, and emboldened me to rephrase the questions for the cricketer and be myself.

I flag the question, 'What do you most believe in?' as an indicative one for helping us ferret out the values we stand for and trustingly protect them in moments of self-doubt or judgement by others.

Your belief could find a home in yourself or in the universe, or in a greater energy that you may or may not call God, in your skills, in your upbringing, in your principles, in your relationships. This faith will be your pathfinder. It will allow you to love life harder and deliver with discipline at jobs people don't trust you with. It will manifest a patience muscle and build it over time. And when it does, you'll rise with the magnanimity of tides and flow freely, like the fragrance of a flower.

## 20

How would
you introduce
yourself with
love?

I have been teaching since I was seventeen years old. And the one life lesson that has stood the test of time, the one that I have always used as an opening life lesson all around the world, is 'Introduce with love'.

Introducing someone with details is one of the easiest things to do. Most people say your name, a couple of accolades here and there, and that's about it. When you ask them, 'Hey! Who are you?' or 'Tell me something about yourself', you'll see that often people start by describing the position they are at, or the work they do. Introducing with love means enjoying the process of making someone aware about something new or something old but in a new manner. Only once you have learnt to do it for yourself can you begin to introduce others with that sense of warmth or depth.

One time, I was speaking at a leadership summit, and before the conference began, I was introduced to this guy from the senior management in the hotel lobby. So I told him, 'It's such a pleasure to meet you. I would love to know more about you.'

He began, 'Well, I am the vice president of the sales division of ———.'

I said, 'Oh, all right. I have never been a VP of anything. Tell me more about yourself.'

He continued, 'I have been the district head of the chapter for ———.'

'Tell me more.'

'I mentor four start-ups that now have a turnover of about ————.'

I spoke to him for twenty minutes and walked away still knowing nothing other than maybe his LinkedIn profile. (Yup! I looked it up later.)

At the conference, I turned to the audience during my session and asked them to write their one-line introduction with love. I saw the same person I had met earlier struggling for over five minutes. Then he penned down these words: 'I feel like a real-life superhero every day.' I asked, 'How so?' He started telling the room that many times, despite the top position he was at, he took out time for all the people in the company and always had their back. He ensured the happiness of his lower management even though it didn't come under his work responsibilities.

A friend of mine, Siddharth Anantharam, said to me once, 'I am someone who will smile at you. Even if you don't smile back at me.' Now how good is that as a preface to knowing someone? Especially in a world where small talk is the defence mechanism of conversations.

Sing it out. Dance it off. Choose what you can to best describe yourself. Every time you get an opportunity to introduce yourself, try not to list out a series of your accomplishments, but rather speak the truth of your being. I want people to say their name with love. The kind of love that makes people sing and shiver, and leaves them startled. I want people to have fun with their introductions, because if the foreword of a book is dead you can't expect the book to be a bestseller.

When I am in a classroom, I ask my students to condense who they are in a statement. And when you finish reading this, try it out for yourself. Try to sit and think, if you had to define yourself in one line with love, what would you say?

## 21

How can you
help make the
world a better
place?

I met Barbarou on the street leading to a Swedish church in Stockholm. I was travelling through Europe, documenting the life lessons of refugees, who were displaced primarily by the conflict in Syria, and the various stakeholders involved in their integration in Europe.

Almost instinctively, as soon as I saw Barbarou, I leaned towards the interviewee who was walking beside me and asked her if she knew the lady in the wheelchair. To my surprise, she did! And so, at a street corner in Sweden, began one of the most heart-warming (and quickest) conversations I have ever had with anyone.

'It might be impolite to ask, but may I know how old you are?' I said hesitatingly.

'Eighty-two. I have managed to see what eighty-two looks like,' replied Barbarou in a thick, slow yet warm voice.

'And what has life taught you? What is the single most important thing that you've learnt in the last eighty-two years?' I asked.

'I had a wonderful marriage and a great career. I was working full-time till I was sixty-six years old. And both my husband and I made sure that we took time out every once in a while to reflect on the way life was going. If we were giving enough time to things that mattered. To evaluate if we were showing people we loved that we cared. It was like our ritual to sit down every so often and take notes from whatever had happened so far. That's how you make life beautiful and create more peace in the world. It might sound time-consuming but it isn't.'

She added, 'And so my life lesson is: Take out time to reflect on what you can do to make the world a better place.'

It was such a profound piece of wisdom spoken with such ease and clarity that it astounded me.

Often, amid travels and lonesome Saturday nights, I think of what Barbarou and her husband have been practising—simple ways to heal the world—almost as a way of life rather than a big boo-ha-ha one-time charity event. There is no 'messiah attitude', just two humble human beings doing what every person can do.

In the glory of our overburdened world, it might never be possible for us to help everyone. But it is definitely within our means to reach out to someone. Anyone. When you avoid an act of kindness, you not only deprive yourself of an opportunity to serve humanity, but also steal from another human being the feeling of gratitude, which will not only comfort him/her but also have the power to touch your spirit. There is no upper limit to how many people you can be kind to or how many people you can love, help or serve. The numbers could run into millions, but don't let that overwhelm you. There is no upper limit but there is a lower limit—one. If you are able to know in your entire lifetime the story of one other human being inside out and can contribute to it in a way that is all and only goodness, you have done the best anyone could do for that human being.

Start small. Nothing fancy. Good intention and courage, the size of a mustard seed, is all you need.

As for me, I did take time out to reflect on how I could make the world a better place, and guess what? I found it. The firsts have always had more meaning than the halfways and the endings. And so, I've found that making things special for people when they are attempting something for the first time makes their world a better place, even if just for a moment. I've decided to be extra nice to people on day one of their job. When I see a sign like 'Opening Day of a Food Truck/Cafe', I go in and buy something; doesn't matter how expensive or cheap. I mark my presence, hold the space for someone else, and add some comfort to their nervousness. Sometimes, good vibes are all that people need to hold on to hope amid all the fear. Good vibes are bravery medals, and I won't forget to put one on people who have earned it by attempting something new that might have held their heart captive for a long, long time. Celebrate the liberation of dreams. And some day, someone will step in to celebrate your beginnings. Make room for it.

## 22

# What do you represent?

I am the kind of interviewee who pays more attention to the question being asked than his own answer. I love it when a question knocks my socks off and makes me relish the exquisite feeling of having never been asked such a thing before. Just a few weeks ago, I was being interviewed over the phone with the usual, expected set of questions: 'How did Project FUEL start?'; 'What do you like more, teaching or lyric writing'; 'What motivates you?', among many others. I have been asked these questions so many times now that the answers are beginning to sound like auto-generated responses from a machine, even though I try to make them sound fresh and new, to the best of my ability, every single time.

Twenty-five minutes into the question-and-answer drill in this particular interview, the person asked in a thoughtful manner, 'Mr Ramola, I am curious to know: What do you represent?' I was caught off guard. I felt as if I was emerging out of a certain level of comfort which I had developed in the course of the interview. I'll be honest in admitting that it felt like an act of mental gymnastics to wrap my mind around the question and surrender to the magnanimity of it with utmost humility. The question made me think about my identity, belongingness, cultural values, belief system, ideologies and virtues. It made me think about my certainties and insecurities.

The interviewer did not ask 'What do you stand for?' or 'What do you want to be remembered for?', which are easier questions to answer. Instead, she asked me what I represent. That question is all-encompassing, and thus, much harder to answer, I feel.

Before I could attempt to construct my own answer, I reached out to what the great African-American poet Maya Angelou had said when asked the question of identity. Reflecting on the visibility her success granted her and the responsibility that came with it, she had said:

> What I represent in fact, what I'm trying like hell to represent every time I go into that hotel room, is myself. People often put labels on people so they don't have to deal with the physical fact of those people. It's easy to say, oh, that's a honkie, that's a Jew, that's a junkie, or that's a broad, or that's a stud, or that's a dude. So you don't have to think: does this person long for Christmas? . . . I refuse that . . . I simply refuse to have my life narrowed and proscribed.

The society we are part of and the culture we are raised in manufactures for us an image of ourselves that must receive a couple of hundred stamps of validation from people who either have little or no contribution in that development. Because of the work we do or the way we look or dress or the place we come from, we are easily categorized into a particular domain of service or facility that we are engaged in or are expected to excel in. This leads to the age-old trouble of labelling.

The great American author and professor Leo Buscaglia wrote extensively on the perils of such labelling; a narrow definition of intelligence and ability, which results in a narrow field of belonging, which in turn casts everyone outside of it as a misfit provided by society, hampering not only personal but spiritual growth. He wrote:

> How many kids have not been educated just because someone pinned a label on them somewhere along the line? Stupid, dumb, emotionally disturbed. I have never known a stupid child. Never! Never! I've only known children and never two alike. Labels are distancing phenomena. They push us away from each other. Black man. What's a black man? I've never known two alike. Does he love? Does he care? What about his kids? Has he cried? Is he lonely? Is he beautiful? Is he happy? Is he giving something to someone? These are the important things..

He further lamented by saying:

> Labels are distancing phenomena—stop using them! And when people use them around you, have the gumption and the guts to say, 'What and who are you talking about because I don't know any such thing.' . . . There is no word vast enough to begin to describe even the simplest of man. But only you can stop it. A loving person won't stand for it. There are too many beautiful things about each human being to call him a name and put him aside.

Although I must have been labelled countless times in the past twenty-seven years of my life, I found the catechism of the interviewer about my choice of what I represent sort of liberating. I loved that I was asked not to validate or expatiate on what people thought of me but rather what I embodied. The opportunity to create my own definition demanded me to reflect on my entire life and speak not only what I felt in my bones but also in my bone marrow—the truth. After much thought and prayer, I whispered into the phone, 'I represent a philosophy of liberation that comes with the acceptance of other people's learnings.' The mere acknowledgement of the fact that someone in some part of the world, irrespective of time zones and transcending the hundreds of centuries that have nurtured humans before me, has been in a situation as familiar as mine and has emerged out of it victorious by learning something reassures me of my own potential to get through whatever it is I am dealing with. Fame can be overwhelming and criticism can be mortifying, love can be confounding and failure can be humbling, but to know and accept the actuality that I am not alone and never have been is soothing on many levels.

I came out of that interview having understood myself better. I explored and found an answer to a question I had never been asked before and one I never felt the need to explore. After that interview, I was convinced this question should be added to the toughest questions list.

Tell me about
a time you made
an assumption
and were proven
wrong

I was of the opinion that our happiness lies outside of us. In people. In experiences. In profits. In success. In other people's satisfaction with us. And therefore, from the early years of my life, nearly up until my twentieth year, I tried to ensure everyone around me was happy with me. It was only after a while, once the social commentary on happiness had bored me to death, that I started to look within and rejoice in my own findings.

I began unearthing clarity over my innate joy. I started paying attention to what made me happy inside and allowed myself to carry that sense of optimism to everything else around me. Some of the people that you are trying to route your happiness through might be deeper in the pit with you. And you have to be cautious of their denseness. People who are unsure about who they are will confuse you about your own identity. Don't be misguided by their doubt, misled by the insecurity and misinformed with their uncertainty.

My previous assumption about happiness also surfaced from the belief that it was a failure to start alone. When you felt you were ready to aim higher but those around you didn't quite see it. To wait endlessly trying to convince others takes up much more time and effort than leading by example. Some people are not ready and perhaps they never will be. If you do things with heart, you'll have to add dollops of patience to that recipe of dreams. Because not everybody will buy into your vision. The world is driven by quantity; quality takes its own time to find admirers. And that process is excruciating, no doubt about it.

I have never seen a flower refusing to bloom because there isn't another flower in the neighbourhood blooming with it. Or a river that demands to see the trajectory of another river deciding its own course. I am yet to come across a leaf that grows enchanted by the company of others on a thread like stem. Or a rock that measures itself against the strength of another stone.

Every element in nature celebrates itself for its entirety. It definitely adds colour and meaning to the collective but never feels reduced by its singularity. Maybe we too can find the courage to begin alone, to bloom in our solitude and yet feel whole.

I hope you can survive it. I hope we all do. To really experience what the other side feels like. I know it exists. We are almost there.

## 24

What lesson
in life took
you the
longest to
learn?

I have been a 'people pleaser' all my life. I have no shame admitting it because I now know better. I am better schooled about the truth that it is indeed impossible to make everyone happy. Even if you are speaking a universal truth like 'the sun rises from the east', you can be rest assured that someone will raise their hand and say it's a conspiracy theory.

I am not sure when this desire to nod to the opinion of others in order to keep them in a blissful state arose within me. Maybe because I did not have close friends in school, I felt agreeing with someone, even when unsure about their standpoint, could help me earn their companionship. Desperation to be seen or heard or to feel valued often leads us to a lane we neither recognize nor belong to. Yet, so many of us stay put because we are irresolute about other possibilities. I sure did stay in a lane like that for a long time. It is a lesson I am still living. Uttering a 'no' or 'stop it' or 'that's not funny' or 'I don't think so' needs a fair amount of moral muscle power.

There is nothing wrong in making others ecstatic if it doesn't come at the cost of your own integrity and sanity. It made me an obsequious, subservient person. I feared showing my emotions, thus compromising my authenticity on many occasions. My classmates labelled me the 'yes man' of our batch.

However, somewhere in my final year of college, it hit me, that big bang of an epiphany. I realized that people are like plants, no matter how much you wish, all you can do for them is provide resources, care and assistance so that they can reach their highest potential. You cannot force them to grow your way. There will be a trait, a behaviour that will pop out like a leaf unforeseen that is not bargained for. The last thing you can offer is that you leave them with hope.

My friend Trisha Ravi's words, which she said on a rickshaw ride back to the hostel, still ring true. We had met a friend whom we thought only took advantage of our affection. She said, 'People really need you until they don't.' I have come to believe it is true. But despite the awareness of its harshness, I choose to love them deeply as long as I have the power to do so. I refuse to let my wholeness be reduced before the waves of time wash away their footprints just because I was expected to serve as a part of their puzzle. In their contentment lies my ability to comfort and cheer. I now know that being polite and courteous is a choice available to me, which I exercise not because I am expected to win over the other person, but because that is who I am. It took some time, but I have moved from the necessity of being liked by everyone to be understood by a handful, hopefully.

Nobel Peace Prize laureate Jody Williams told me in a conversation, 'Life is not a popularity contest.' A lesson she said, unlike me, she learnt at the tender age of thirteen. While at junior high school, her best friend at the time kissed a boy in her class. The boy, however, proclaimed to everyone that he had had his way with her. He cooked and spiced up the story to prove he was cool. He did that at the cost of the girl's reputation and trust. Jody said, 'In my little peanut brain,

I learnt that very day that people will inflate, deflate, conflate facts to suit their interest. So instead of trying to please them, try to stick to your truth.'

I wish I too had learnt this early on in life. I would have saved myself from massive heartbreaks, disastrous disappointment and, not to mention, the iceberg of expectations. Nonetheless, some life lessons, I suppose, morph into new circumstances to drive the point home, until we really get it. If you are someone who is always late, your life will repeatedly present this fact and its learnings to you, hoping you do better. Whether you were late in fifth grade for hockey practice or at work every morning now, certain lessons really measure up to reveal how much progress you have made. It is like repeating a class just because you did not qualify the first time. You are detained in the subject, and all you have to do is prep well for the next time.

## 25

Are
you
successful?

In the summer of 2007, my sister decided to enrol in an English-speaking course for three months. Our school vacations stretched out for three months ahead of us and our parents urged us to do something meaningful with them. My sister was convinced; she needed a better hand at the language and therefore rang up to fix an interview with the coaching centre. I, however, spoke considerably well for my age, but agreed to accompany her for the interview. At the centre, she went first and answered a few questions. Just for kicks, I decided to give it a shot myself to experience what questions the interviewer had for us.

The man who ran the centre was a tall man with a husky voice tone and deadpan expression. I must have exuded some level of confidence, as the first and only question he asked me was, 'Are you successful?' Now, mind you, I was sixteen years old and a bit taken aback with the outright sharpness of the question. Success to me, until then, was something you worked towards. It was a concept sold as a vision, a goal one had to achieve to feel content, a destination one had to arrive at in order to feel accomplished. But as that question simmered in my mind, I felt something most introspective and gratifying within me. I acknowledged that I did feel successful. For the first time in my life, I found the time and courage to admit that my definition of having made it wasn't externally influenced but rather internally formulated.

Over the years, this question has generated a flood of diverse responses from people. Whether you think you are successful or not depends entirely upon your definition of success. Does the favourable outcome of an effort you invested time in make you feel accomplished? Or does your triumph find its oxygen in the day-to-day mundane routine? The answers are as many as there are shades of people in the world. But it helps to pause and ruminate over what tools and benchmarks you have set for yourself to feel you have profited over this affair called life.

In my experience, it always helps to find achievement in the small acts of progress. That way the bigger wins will seem grander and the small ones won't go amiss. A friend and inspiring change-maker named Benje Williams once shared an incredible story about a time in his working life that consolidated the thought I shared above.

Benje grew up in America and went to Kenya for an international education project. He said nothing good came out of it. It was a million-dollar fail in many ways, except that one woman got a chance to pursue a graduate degree in Canada. That was about it. Everyone was pretty disappointed with the outcome and soon moved on to other things in life. Benje, too, settled in Pakistan and started his organization, Amal Academy. Three years later, the same woman who had gone to Canada because of the education project returned to her community in Kenya. She became a role model for other parents who encouraged their children to go to school and learn. Her story was an instrument of change for quality education and participation in learning for both parents and young adults—which was the initial goal of the million-dollar project that tanked. Benje confessed to me that the experience taught him to embrace small beginnings.

While to rejoice over bagging a project is only fair, even to have made a great presentation for it is an act of celebration. The food on the plate might be something you relish, but even managing to source the ingredients to make it is a success. We are often engrossed in thinking only about the final outcome. Most certainly, that results in deep disappointment when it is not favourable.

Some people pick pain over pleasure, hardship over happiness and struggle over satisfaction. It all boils down to your choice in any given moment of life. Choice, followed by reaction, is the exposition of success. And perhaps, just for today, success looks like an afternoon nap. A book read between cursive dreams, dozing in and out of the parallel universes of imagination. Sunshine as the halo and the cool breeze as your soulkeeper. Just in this moment, conceivably, the reward is to hang the cape and dance to a life unchoreographed. It's like drinking an iced lemonade, sitting on the kitchen countertop, chatting with your mother or humming alongside your partner. It's in having made it so far despite the odds.

For all one knows, this is why Ralph Waldo Emerson wrote:

To laugh often and much; to win the respect of intelligent people and the affection of children; to earn the appreciation of honest critics and endure the betrayal of false friends; to appreciate the beauty; to find the best in others; to leave the world a bit better, whether by a healthy child, a garden patch or a redeemed social condition; to know even one life has breathed easier because you have lived. This is to have succeeded!

## 26

What
makes
you
weep?

We all are reservoirs of pain. Or will be at some point in our lives, if we have lived fully—embraced the scars, the bruises and the brutalities. The bullying, the banishment, the hurt and the unresolved matters of the heart all adding to it drop by drop. There seems to be a well that never runs dry, only gets inaccessible at times. Unrequited love, demotion from a dream job, betrayal from a loved one or sometimes simply phantom misery, the kind you feel by observing someone else, someone you don't even know personally.

I weep at the sight of a couple fighting in public. I swear, almost every single time I notice two people, probably married, fighting on the streets, my eyes well up. I can feel the ache rising. What about it makes me emotional? I have thought about it. Usually, in situations like these, the man has the upper hand of being abusive or irrationally violent. The woman seems to be soaking it all in. Embarrassed and agonized, I harmonize with the helplessness of the person. Helplessness, yes, that is the other strong component of my outburst. Apart from this, heartfelt goodbye videos contribute to my tears. But I have learnt to not apologize or feel sorry about this attribute.

The holiness of happiness is great but the catharsis of weeping is irreplaceable. Growing up, my grandmother would often tell me to let go in an emotional situation, but to shed a handful of tears before doing so. It washes the pain further away, she would declare, and douses the fire of anger.

Many people live under the thick pretence of being strong. Weeping or crying (I think the former is more intense) is an act of bravery. One may weep not only instigated by the negative or unfortunate occurrences, but also out of joy. That is why when people win a lottery or are given a big surprise, they weep with exhilaration. People also weep when they are extremely angry. It is a universal emotion, and anyone who makes you feel small because you express it should be sent on a solo trip out of your life.

When we finally find a moment, we can almost acknowledge what stirs the agony within us. And the least we can do is allow our eyes to moisten, our cheekbones to soften and our shoulders to lighten up. Devoid of bitterness or rage, weeping is a peculiar yet familiar emotion that needs to pass through us and requires our permission to do so. A permission we are most afraid to issue.

Weeping is the cheapest therapist there is. You just have to figure out how to do it appropriately. And if it is permission you are looking for, consider this statement as my word for it. You have permission to weep! A few drops, a pint-sized outburst or a natural-disaster-level flood of tears—all of it! You have the warrant to wail and howl with tears if you like. The only promise you need to make is that you will come out of it. It should only be a season in the nature of emotion, not a way of life. It should not suck you into the black hole of never-ending grief or comfort. It has to be your armour, not the victim card. If you can promise me that, you have the licence to weep. I am sure you'll feel better. And if you don't, we will together trace the words of preacher F.W. Boreham and ask what the hell he meant when he proclaimed: 'The eyes, cleansed by weeping, have obtained a clearer vision of life's profound mystery and beneficent discipline.'

I wish you good cries. Ones where your tears are stamps of assurance that you have touched the chord of someone's life, and the only music that comes out is the one that will mend you. They will tuck you into bed gently. On your cheeks, good cries will be the showers of first rain. You will be able to smell the skin. Good cries will be the evidence of a good life.

## 27

When was the
last time you
wished for
something
to last
forever?

When we were young, my mother would take my sister and me to the woods and give us an hour or so to roam freely in the bewildering beauty of nature and familiarize ourselves with the wonder of the forest. On most days, the task assigned to us was to name as many trees as possible. Both my sister and I, with that powerful challenge, would investigate and name tree after tree. We would scan the short ones, the tall ones, the ones birds agreed to lease a house on, the fruit-bearing ones, the barren and parched ones, the ones that looked like they had been awaiting a monsoon for eternity, and the scarily deformed ones. The only rule was that we had to choose the same set of trees and arrive at a common agreement of naming one. As kids, agreeing to one name was the hard part. We would soon turn into mini lawyers, negotiating the validation of an opinion and being thrashed inadvertently by the facts of the other. The conversation would then take shape and morph us into poets searching for metaphors to substantiate our recommendations.

A few hours later, my mother would show up to witness our process. We would then take her for a meet and greet with the trees we had befriended. This act alone was the most nerve-racking one, buzzing with excitement. As if not only our mother but even the forest was curious to hear about our creative conclusions.

Both of us would take turns to introduce her to the trees. We had to, of course, tell her the name but also why we had decided to name it that. What characteristics did we take into consideration, what features caught our eye, which decision did we have to debate among other things to find a common solution?

My mother would patiently listen as we tried to enlighten her with the logic and reasoning of our little brains. The names we gave the trees were a representation of many things: people we loved, those we didn't, people who intimidated us with their size and presence, names we had heard in fictional stories, those that coloured our memories, those from television shows, and other mumbo-jumbo phantasmagorical ones.

And although the whole exercise was about trees in a forest, it certainly did reveal a lot about us. Yup! My mother should have been a psychology professor. The seeds of observation, perception, compassion, peacebuilding, conflict resolution and presentation for us were sown in those very walks.

There are many days I wish this game of my childhood could stretch itself over a lifetime. But I suppose adulthood is the interest you pay on the loan of childhood that life lends you.

There is another incident I am mustering up the courage to share with you. It was amusing and silly, and one whose embarrassment I hope doesn't last a lifetime.

It is a middle-class viewpoint, I guess, that you believe the best dishes are made and the most delicious snacks laid out only when guests visit. One time, both my sister and I stood gaping as our mother placed a buffet full of fruits and mouth-watering sweets before visiting relatives.

Throughout their conversations, we only waited for them to leave. As the moment arrived, we walked them out, bid goodbye and then ran back inside like malnourished, starving children. We jumped at each snack item like we had not seen food before. Unfazed, while we displayed our wild animal behaviour, to our embarrassing shock, the relatives came back with our parents to pick up a bag they had forgotten. My parents could have decided to give us up for adoption that day.

Thank God they didn't. Or on one of those forest visits, my mother could have conveniently left us to name trees and grow up to be versions of Mowgli from *The Jungle Book*.

## 28

If your life was
a cycle of seasons,
which season
are you
in now?

Bone-chilling winter cold. A quaint autumn of shedding old leaves, letting go of people, but joyous with the anticipation of a bloom ahead. Cold snow caves awaiting bonfire warmth. Waves of moody monsoon. Gloomy affairs in the middle of summer. The parched heat of end June. Sunshine with passing clouds. Spring with the jolt of new possibilities. In a downpour of romantic love. A storm of uncertainties and anxiety, disciplining everything random into a routine. A bit of winter freeze, longing winds of change. On the brink of a new autumn, carrying the reminiscence of the old one. The flourishing innocence of new buds or the acceptance of decayed leaves. A season of aesthetic divinity or a dawn of new colours. A maybe-winter or a hell-yes autumn. Summer sweat gifted under the bright sun in the golden sky or a mild red face bitten by the agonizing frost. The unbuttoned breeze of May or the dense fog of a hazy January. Awaiting rescue or enjoying falling. The odd, uneven, coarse August rain or a dreamy September afternoon. Overcast with doubts or suffocated with the darkness of expectations. Fighting the constant drizzle or getting drenched in the outpour. The green of spring or the mustard yellow of autumn.

If your life was a cycle of seasons, which season are you in now?

Make a note of the 'now' in the question. Update yourself with an inner weather report by scanning the season you are breathing in. Like all things true, seasons too are transient. If you are stuck in the rain, look for an umbrella. If it's bright and sunny, go out and get some Vitamin D. I read somewhere that nothing in nature blooms all year long. It was one of the most comforting things to read, especially at a time when three major projects of mine were cancelled or postponed. I did not feel healthy and chaotic emotions hung over my head all day long. But I knew acknowledging how I felt was the way out. Running away from the storm is like inviting it to chase you until the dead end, till it wears you out. Ignoring the bliss of spring is to trick yourself into ungratefulness.

Some friends of mine juggle between multiple seasons in a single day. It's amusing, because that takes courage and talent. Courage to battle the tough times, show up for the sizzling ones and leave aside the lukewarm ones. What they definitely don't do is feel miserable about the season they are in. They are simply aware of its presence. And aware that they are passing through, not staying in it. Sharing feelings with others can help someone else be free of misery, reminding them that they are not alone.

The other interesting observation is what different things mean to different people. Winter may connote a peaceful time of leisure and curling into peace for one, and a depressed state of being for another. Autumn might be dreary and taxing for somebody who is dealing with a loss, and a time to shed the unnecessary for somebody wanting to shape a better tomorrow. The seasons of our lives are the measuring tape of our evolution. Helping us mark our own temperatures, regulating our own climatic conditions, and eventually nudging us to settle for what is the best.

## 29

What doesn't
matter to
you any
more?

Through all the twenty-seven winters my life has seen, I have always carried a warm summer sun within me. I no longer feel scared of a bad mood or a terrible situation. I know they will pass. It doesn't matter how grave everyone makes you believe you must be. Every decision you make is coloured by how you feel in a particular moment or phase in your life. Feelings are the most impermanent of things in this overall evanescent existence. You will feel something today, and at the turn of a new day or a defining incident or even as a new week, month or year approaches, you will feel deeply different. Don't hold on to these dwindling concoctions of emotions with all your might. They were, have been and will be brief—like the history of time. You can allow yourself to be absorbed by them, but they should not consume you. To escape them is impossible, and to evolve with them is intelligence. Do not use them like barricades, shielding you from new opportunities, or build them like walls, one over the other, until you lose sight of those who still hold the power to love you or forgive you.

Use them like maps, to navigate new territories, giving yourself time to comprehend the complexities of new relationships. Flow with them like a stream of water, carving

151

its path with exploration, blazing in every drop and full of grace in its actions.

In the economy of living, feelings are like currencies. And like every currency, they have their own prejudices to fight, their own perceptions to encounter and their own stock of power play to deal with. You grow and glow with your stake of currency. Their value changes with every gesture and reaction. But they are here to serve you, not control you. If you remember their imperativeness then they don't weigh heavy on your decisions.

It is only with this epiphany that I have been able to forgive people who have hurt me the most. To the degree that I can work with them professionally or look them in the eye. Or be in the same room without vengeance or revenge burning within me. It is not that the feelings that existed earlier have been buried, but rather they have been resolved intentionally to make space for other feelings. Hopefully, better ones. It doesn't matter to me any more when people bitch about somebody they dislike now but come to love them in a couple of months. Similarly, in a few years, they might not be able to stand the sight of someone they love today.

The other important thing to be aware of is that feelings are indispensable. There is no antonym for this fact. The opposite of being emotional is being logical, the opposite of insanity is sanity. What is the opposite of 'feel'? It can't be 'unfeel'. Because you cannot feel a sense of 'unfeel'; that is paradoxical. Love the transience of feelings and live with their distinctive need to feel important. Feelings are in the pursuit of becoming better, and, pray, we are too.

## 30

What is the
one thing you
are in denial
about in
your life?

I feel really good about myself now. But it's been a long journey to this place. Growing up, I hadn't necessarily bought into the idea of liking myself. When the majority tells you that you don't belong or that you are weird or that you don't matter, it's hard to not be consumed by it in the moment. That thing is painful and embarrassing. What I have tried doing, though, and the thing that saved my self-esteem during that time, was to build a counter-narrative to their story. If they said I sounded like a kid or a girl, my reply would be, 'Maybe I do. But listen to what I have to offer in the voice of that kid or girl.' And I did my homework. I was loaded with fascinating tales, epic anecdotes, rich experiences; I read books and earned my skills as a raconteur. Whenever someone sat down to have a conversation with me, I ensured that they walked away feeling better or entertained or informed about something. Eventually, that narrative outshone the other things being said about me. My narrative made me win and won them over.

If you spend all your time trying to edit other people's story of you then you will be left with hardly any time to construct your own. Be the author of your own story, not the editor of their interpretation. I constantly negotiated the truth amid the facts. The fact was I did lack a baritone voice in comparison to the other boys whose voice had cracked by the time they were fifteen. So what? I knew I had to speak up irrespective of that and make myself heard. In order to achieve this, I participated in the school assembly, every alternate week or so. I stood in front of the entire school and read out the morning news, the thought for the day or a poem. Over time, I became a good orator and was appointed the official school debater. Representing my ideas, vouching for them when no one else would, is a virtue I have built over the years. One thing I have refused to accept are the stories about myself others have offered to me. Their versions were partly amusing and true but never fully accurate.

Years ago, in a school that I was teaching at, during a round of introductions with the students, I came across a boy with an injured eye. As I approached him, I could hear the snickering, giggling and name-calling he was subjected to by some of his classmates. The boy was infuriated. He almost punched some of them. I recognized his frustration as I could see myself in his situation. His anger was a reflection of my own emotions during my schooldays. So I walked up to the stage holding his hand and told everyone he was one of the most talented people in that classroom. The class, along with the boy, looked perplexed. They had never seen him as someone with value, let alone talent. I asked the boy, 'Do you study like everyone else for exams?' He replied with a resounding yes! 'Do you play a sport like everyone else?' 'Yes, I do,' he responded. After a series of six or seven questions, I told him and the class, 'Everything that you do with two eyes, he does with just one. And that too without any arrogance. Shouldn't we be counting our blessings that he doesn't make us feel inferior because of his skills and superpower?' Before

I could finish my sentence, the boy hugged me and started to cry. I teared up as well. I knew I had been able to offer him an empowering narrative; one that might help him look others in the eye instead of lowering his gaze with shame. He later told me a cricket ball had damaged his cornea during a game in his neighbourhood. In all these years, he had not forgiven the boy who was bowling that day. 'I think I am ready to speak to him again,' he shared.

You can be in denial about anything. It doesn't have to be a story or a perception that others have about you. It can be that your marriage is more troubled than you realize. That your children are mature enough to handle their own decisions, or that you need to quit a job instead of telling yourself it will get better. Ignoring a problem is not solving it. Denial often clogs our ability to take a learned decision. I won't lie, though, it's not easy to welcome what we have been skilfully repudiating. It's hard, agreed, but worth it nonetheless.

## 31

What would
happen if love
and trust switched
roles for a day
in your life?

I may be wrong, but I have come to believe that we love the person we trust by default, but not the other way around. We don't always end up trusting the people we love. I have many relationships in which I genuinely, authentically and steadily love the person. But we have reservations about telling them a secret or something deeply personal. The reasons are fairly diverse—the person is a loudmouth, their insecurities often override the conversation, they may use it against you in an argument later, or that they are simply not ready to absorb what you are sharing.

Lack of this virtue doesn't make them bad people or subtract their value. We love them for who they are and what they add to our lives. But the question comes up: If both love and trust switched places for a day in your life, what would it lead to? Some people say that the day would be as normal as any other. Nothing would change. Others have a starker reaction, 'Oh! I will have a field day with too much explaining to do.' The question is also a tough one because it urges us to differentiate between the ones we love and the ones we trust, or the ones we endow with both these qualities.

Does over-trusting diminish the significance of love? Is it better to trust someone than to love them? Is it hard to find people in the world today with whom you can experience both? What are the repercussions of loving someone first and then arriving at the trust station? Can you really love without trusting the other person? There are many thoughts that cross my mind. I haven't been able to fully formulate a stand on it. Trust is earned through actions while love can be sporadic and irrational. Is that why it's easy to fall back in love but difficult to trust again once it has been bruised? If there is a precondition of trust in love, does it signify that merely love is not enough? Conditioned love is not really love, is it?

The Internet is an ocean on the theme, with plenty of write-ups and myriad perspectives. I wonder what makes you feel better: to be trusted or to be loved? Love can be a one-way street but trust is a highway. Drivers on both sides have to be mindful of the responsibility. Does that make trust more cumbersome in our already complicated lives?

In all the years of collecting life lessons, I have analysed a pattern. The world doesn't lack love; there is an abundance of it. The ways to express it are muddled and scattered. But there is a deficit of trust. Thousands of life lessons originate from a breach of trust, advising others to be careful or cautious about whom they bestow their trust upon. There are others that label trust as being the hard reward in a tough relationship.

This brings me back to my question: What would happen if trust and love switched roles for a day in your life? Your answer can help the rest of us juggling with our own puzzlement on the subject. If nothing else, it will help you assimilate what matters more to you in all the relationships you hold close to your heart.

There is a knock at the door. It might be your healing showing up finally, tired by the maps that wore it out, or by the streets full of mirages. Or it might have been hurt while returning to a safe shore, this time with sharpened weapons. Attempting another assassination of what you believe is possible. There is a knock at the door of your heart. If you don't open it, you will never know. The question is, will you be okay with it?

## 32

Where does
your inspiration
find its roots?

Maya Angelou, the great African-American actor, dancer, poet, novelist, activist, producer and speaker, once said in an interview that she had a painting by the artist Phoebe Beasley of a group of women, which she calls 'Sister Sookie's Funeral'. There are about nine women in that painting,. who Angelou felt looked like her grandmother's prayer meeting group. Whenever she felt obliged to do something, she would look at the painting, at the empty chair in the centre of it, and think, 'Now what would Grandma do?' Angelou said, 'As I look at the painting, I can almost hear her say, "Now, sister, you know what's right. Just do right."' And that helped her write every single time she was invited to present a commencement speech, write a book or perform a poem for the President's inaugural ceremony.

Art in any form can inspire you and set you free from the shackles of fear, insecurity, doubt and timidity. When I go to colleges, school campuses or institutions to teach, the one thing I ask my students to remember is to take a piece of art—anything—like a painting by Picasso, a poem by Langston Hughes, a performance by Marina Abramovic, and to make it their own. By this I don't mean buy it or print a copy off the Internet and replace the artist's name with yours. I mean you should take a piece of art and use it to become a better person, a better scholar, a better voice, a better writer, a better restaurateur, a better chef—whatever it is that you are hoping to achieve. Once you do that, you will realize your story has strength, no matter what you are speaking about.

If you look around yourself, you will notice there is enough craftsmanship and abundant inventiveness available to harness; to get on a stage, to speak to a crowd, however large. You will be able to speak, because for you, someone has already said the right thing.

Our life itself provides us countless ropes to cling on to when climbing the mountain of motivation and creativity from the dreary valley of humdrum. Poet and novelist Rainer Maria Rilke wrote in his semi-autobiographical book, *The Notebooks of Malte Laurids Brigge:*

> For the sake of a few lines one must see many cities, men and things. One must know the animals, one must feel how the birds fly and know the gesture with which the small flowers open in the morning. One must be able to think back to roads in unknown regions, to unexpected meetings and to partings which one has long seen coming; to days of childhood that are still unexplained . . . But one must also have been beside the dying, one must have sat beside the dead in the room with the open window and the fitful noises.

Inspiration often gets misunderstood as a prerequisite toolbox that can be accessed by and is meant only for creative people or artists. Nothing could be further from the truth. It doesn't matter if you are a salesperson, a corporate employee, a housewife or an old retired servant, inspiration fuels each one of us to live more passionately, explore our curiosity and keep our engines in motion. Our gardens, bookshelves, poems, stories, dinner presentations, living-room décor, walls and personalities emerge and expand with stimulation. Artist Agnes Martin illustrates it best by saying, 'An inspiration is a happy moment that takes us by surprise. It is an untroubled state of mind. Of course, we know that an untroubled state of mind cannot last, so we say that inspiration comes and goes, but it is there all the time waiting for us to be untroubled again. We can therefore say that it is pervasive.'

There is a need in us to feel inspired. It makes us seekers. It allows us to create, find and follow role models, pin up mood boards and create vision maps. And if we do find one (or many), it validates the truth that we find a reflection of ourselves in someone else's story. Maybe then our need to feel inspired springs from the desire to know that someone showed courage before us. Courage that we want in order to fulfil a goal of our own. Life, as I see it, is like a see-saw. Allowing yourself to feel inspired by someone's actions or ideas is to let someone go up on the see-saw. The purpose is to then radiate what you learn to the extent that you become a role model for others, so that others can allow you to go up. But first, we must enter the playground!

## 33

What does pain that no longer hurts morph into?

Acceptance. Unshaken smiles. Memories that don't affect you any more. Divine strength. Prolonged silence. Life lessons. Courage. Art. Wisdom. Empathy. Insanity. Cautioned living. Eccentricity. A ticket to the past with no regret or fear. Understanding.

These are the range of answers offered by people in response to this question.

I would like to add: drunk texts, stomach aches, unexpected ugly crying. And two medium-sized, thin-crust pizzas, to begin with.

Last fall, I was there. In the pit of pain, with hardly any room to even turn around. A friend I blindly trusted knocked me out with accusations that were a result of his own overthinking and bias. Yet, there was work to be done, conferences to speak at, people to greet, videos to record and social media status quo to maintain. My deep hurt found it harder to resolve itself in the public spotlight and more so, because I did not deserve it in the first place. I was so tempted to call the person to offer a piece of my mind and find closure. Until Apoorva called to say, 'Their act WAS the closure. What would trying to show them your anger do? It won't help at all. It will just allow you to stoop down to that person's level as you'll abuse, ask for justifications and feel better that you made them feel bad for what they did.'

Suddenly, my resentment did not aspire for a crime-thriller-like revenge, rather I found myself in a state of determined peace. I called the person and, instead of giving him a taste of his own medicine, said, 'I heard you. It was hurtful and could be better communicated. I will need some time to heal and I want you to not bother me until then.'

Months later, as I write this chapter, I have an update to share: The person turned around and apologized. I am able to collaborate with him again on assignments that could have easily been shelved because I didn't want to see his face again. I have learnt during this phase that for me, pain that no longer hurts morphs into grace. However, I am not the Dalai Lama, and there were dark days when I felt like punching the person in the face and shaming him among all our common friends. The eventual grace helped me restore my sanity and not lose my calm. Even our pain is a privilege, and we need to be cautious about who gets to see us broken and exposed. Certainly not the person who caused it in the first place.

From my experience, I have learnt that pain can be easy to get rid of; it's the sadness that lingers and is the most damaging. Perhaps that is why I get terribly physically sick when I am emotionally unwell. Otherwise, my immune system is stronger than tungsten. Let's unmistakably evaluate what we remember about the pain. The person who inflicted it upon us or how it made us feel? We may find a clue in the answer to renew our strength.

To live is to be both benefitted and bruised. And maybe bruised a bit more than benefitted for some. The bitterness of a particular incident that harmed us quite often guides our whole narrative. One can taste tension in the words, spitefulness in the coping strategies and the vibe of something that remains unresolved in the vengeance.

## 34

What lie has
convinced you
enough to live
it like a truth?

The search for truth is part of the human longing for a morally fulfilled life, but it is arguably a painful and an unpleasant process. Some truths are better negotiated for a comforting lie. A lie that either assists in damage control or becomes a perennial source of hope in times of despair. It's a lie worth believing, because is there anything like the absolute truth? It evolves differently for different people.

Like when they tell you, 'It only gets better.' No, it doesn't. In fact, it gets worse, weird, scary, awesome and a lot of other things but not better. We need to buy into this belief so that we don't crumble under the agony of a fatal future. It could apply to the facts about our careers, relationships, personalities, among other things that we are aware of but have chosen to cover up with soothing lies.

A friend of mine quipped in response to this question, 'Whatever happens, happens for good', a lie she has been talked into. But it is soul satisfying. What else if not this? When you have been laid off, dumped or have met with a horrible accident, to hear that there is an unknown yet bigger plan at work that will lead to fruition is reassuring. Or we might succumb to the suffering and give up. Another line that often surfaces is, 'Money is everything.' Those who have experienced even a small dose of life's ultimate reality know this is far from the truth, yet we are urged to participate in an Olympic sprint so that we can accumulate more.

There are other lies that are more harmful than the ones listed above. I know people who stay in abusive relationships, living the illusion of a perfect love life in their heads. They know what is happening to them is not right or just, but the truth is too much to lug around so they tranquilize themselves with everything else. It's a lie they want to believe because it's remedying, it doesn't shake the norm or stir a conflict. The anti-racism fight, gender parity and the battle for LBGTQ rights have suffered in many parts of our society due to the comforting lie of religious beliefs, societal dictum and cultural restrictions. Growing up in middle-class patriarchal India, I often encounter women giving up their dreams of being independent because they have bought into the lie that this is how it is supposed to be and one cannot do anything about it. Gender equality is a smoke screen. Equal pay, the right to be heard and financial stability are part of a distant dream that lies across the walls they are confined within.

I am part of a collective called the Wise Wall Project, run by Project FUEL, that aims to document, design and strengthen the wisdom of rural communities and marginalized villages through art. In 2018, for the second edition of the project, we travelled to Khati, a village located in the foothills of the Pindhari glacier in Uttarakhand. Khati, despite a rich history of culture and traditions, faces multiple challenges, like requiring four modes of transport and a trek to reach it! There is no electricity, network or Internet.

We stayed in the village for over a month, far from Internet connectivity, updates and news about civilization. After the project concluded, when I trekked down from Khati and heard a car honk, I was overwhelmed. Being in the village was like living in an alternate world, back in time. Later that evening, I switched on my phone after a month. There were 1400 WhatsApp messages, 814 emails and countless social media notifications. Most emails began with the words 'time sensitive' or 'urgent'. I joked with my colleagues about whether the people who had written a 'time sensitive' email in block letters a month ago were still alive. That life goes on and I am dispensable was the toughest lesson to digest. Even though I know that I am loved, it was a hard pill to swallow that the world managed well in my absence. And still very humbling.

Life, fortunately or unfortunately, doesn't come with a manual. People should know that the world is big and people are mean sometimes. That it gets better and tougher. That things you need the most cost more. And commodities are not the only things with price tags. They should be tutored about the realities of a heartbreak. And about how lonely it gets on certain Saturday nights. That some days you will have a stack of letters but no address to post them to. That some secrets will find their way to more ears than you imagined. And some dreams are fragile. That is why we need to construct our own versions of truth. Truth that is abstract but comforting.

'All truth is simple . . . is that not doubly a lie?' wrote Friedrich Nietzsche. From time to time, we are quizzed by entangled circumstances to choose our truths and construct our lies. When the threat is too high to stay neutral and the responsibility even higher to make an informed decision, the bigger question is, what lie qualifies as the truth you are convinced by?

## 35

What is
your favourite
word?

There is a word in Garhwali, a dialect spoken in my mountainous culture. The word is '*khud*', and it is consciously used when the longing for a beloved rises to an unimaginable level. Loosely, it can be translated to 'deeply missing someone', but it doesn't have a direct or an apt translation in another language. The word 'khud' in Hindi means 'self', and in Garhwali it signifies 'to miss someone to a degree where you forget yourself'. The potency and passion of that missing is what the word depicts. It's a word I like because it doesn't trivialize the torment of someone's absence to a mere 'thinking about you' sentiment, but takes it a notch higher.

There are other words I like—'butterfly', for the simple joy of how it rolls off the tongue each time you utter it. The freedom in 'fly'; the very pronunciation of the word is impromptu yet coordinated. But my most favourite word is 'constellation'. Whenever I am struggling to convey a certain emotion in a conversation, presentation, research report or a poem, the word 'constellation' becomes my refuge. I often curl my back against the world with it.

People wonder how answering what your favourite word is could be among the toughest questions. But to me, it seems imperative that we discover a word that ignites our bones and magnifies our spirit. Words are the cornerstone of survival. In the trenches of a melody, a poet puts in a word and the lyric becomes a chant, an anthem, a lullaby and a war cry. You can string them around and make someone weep. Arrange them artistically and arrive at a joke that never gets old. Words are the tools that make everyone an artist. To communicate, and to communicate well, is to create organic art. Something we all engage in.

Identifying your favourite word helps so that when you stumble upon it in a book or an Instagram quote or even when you hear someone use it in a sentence, you can feel the serendipity of its familiarity. It's like seeing a recognizable face in a crowd. That's another word I like, 'serendipity', which means finding interesting or valuable things by chance.

Your favourite word might be a catchphrase people hear you use often. It rings a bell as soon as it's spoken in a tone and texture that is purely yours. Your favourite word could even be something you heard someone say but never knew the meaning of. It can even be 'fuck', given the versatility of its application. Many people recommend it as a handy favourite word.

People often misinterpret the power of words by limiting their usage to writers, novelists, poets, essayists and researchers. They help us express our pain, declare our meal choices, and if we 'get the right word, and not its second cousin', we may be able to condense a thought into something tangible. As Mark Twain said, 'The difference between the almost right word and the right word is really a large matter. 'Tis the difference between the lightning bug and the lightning.'

Go out there and find a favourite word. There are nearly 20 million words in the world, and that is a conservative estimate. You can pick a word from an endangered language or a dialect your grandparents spoke; you can tickle the world with it or you can use it to mesmerize.

When I need a sacred reminder on the dynamism of words, I often find myself reading heartfelt letters on the incredible online platform 'Letters of Note', curated by archivist and author Shaun Usher.

Here's one I bookmarked for the sheer brilliance and advocacy it commands.

In 1934, a New York-based copywriter by the name of Robert Pirosh quit his well-paid job and headed for Hollywood, determined to begin his dream career as a screenwriter. When he arrived, he gathered the names and addresses of as many directors, producers and studio executives as he could find, and sent them what is surely one of the greatest, most effective cover letters ever to be written; a letter which secured him three interviews, one of which led to his job as a junior writer at MGM. Fifteen years later, screenwriter Robert Pirosh won an Academy Award for Best Original Screenplay for his work on the war film *Battleground*. A few months after that, he also won a Golden Globe.

Dear Sir: I like words. I like fat buttery words, such as ooze, turpitude, glutinous, toady. I like solemn, angular, creaky words, such as straitlaced, cantankerous, pecunious, valedictory. I like spurious, black-is-white words, such as mortician, liquidate, tonsorial, demi-monde. I like suave 'V' words, such as Svengali, svelte, bravura, verve. I like crunchy, brittle, crackly words, such as splinter, grapple, jostle, crusty. I like sullen, crabbed, scowling words, such as skulk, glower, scabby, churl. I like Oh-Heavens, my-gracious, land's-sake words, such as tricksy, tucker, genteel, horrid. I like elegant, flowery words, such as estivate, peregrinate, elysium, halcyon. I like wormy, squirmy, mealy words, such as crawl, blubber, squeal, drip. I like sniggly, chuckling words, such as cowlick, gurgle, bubble and burp. I like the word screenwriter better than copywriter, so I decided to quit my job in a New York advertising agency and try my luck in Hollywood, but before taking the plunge I went to Europe for a year of study, contemplation and horsing around. I have just returned and I still like words. May I have a few with you?

Robert Pirosh
385 Madison Avenue
Room 610
New York
Eldorado 5-6024

## 36

# Do you belong?

The 'other messages' folder of my Instagram profile is my therapist. I receive some of the most heart-warming compliments, words of encouragement and personal stories on it. Whenever I am feeling low and have some time on hand, I dive into it, head first, to resurrect my confidence. There is a message I revisit often, sent by a girl I do not know. But having scanned her profile, I know she is a working professional, loves to read books and aspires to attend a Coldplay concert once in her lifetime. Social media has made us all astrologers. Feeds are the new horoscope, and posts the cosmic stars of identity.

Anyway, I refer to her because she sent me a message that hit home and was an apt reminder of what I subconsciously know. She wrote, 'You seem like the luckiest person in the world. Travelling all around the world with your suitcase of stories, but there is always room for more. Talking to complete strangers and them treating you like you are one of them. That feeling of belonging must be amazing, right? I can't tell you how enchanting your journey looks like to me.' To me too. It is still enchanting and awe-inspiring. I know it sounds very narcissistic to call your own story inspiring but anyone who thinks otherwise can go take a hike into a cactus.

When I arrived, for the first time, at the question, 'Do you belong?', I had so many more questions to ask in response to it.

Belong where? To whom? To life or this job or the person I am dating? The thought ran on like wildfire. Eventually, I could get to answering it with 'Finally, yes!' And then another voice added, 'Not always.' I hardly had any friends in school. I was academically brilliant, always in the top three. I would qualify for representing my school at quiz competitions, debates and anchor ceremonies. Yet, I did not have a friend-friend I could latch on to as my own. The kind you share your bench and your tiffin box with. I hoped for people to like me but I secretly knew I did not belong in their gangs. I was shy, not very mischievous, and they always typecast me as someone weird or different.

Over time, as I owned my story and belonged to myself, I earned newer friends. Enough to start a reality show. I often joke with my friends that I will soon start a lucky list on every New Year's Eve of people who have made it to the next year. They will have special privileges and benefits. Of course, it's a joke. I wouldn't be able to breathe one moment if someone decided to do the same to me and eliminated me from their list. There are so many shades and parts of my survival that are routed through each person I know. This sense of security is the litmus test for knowing I belong to them and they belong to me. In their company, I don't have to be cool or wise or intellectual or funny. I just have to be myself, and whatever colour of emotion I am feeling in that moment. No small talk, dirty joke or debate is required to fill in the silence. One of the greatest moments of life is to be surrounded by all those you love and be bothered by none. In school, I felt the need to constantly prove that I was worthy, realizing only much later that it was a fantastic way to chip away at my worth.

The same scenario played out at a production house I worked at in the initial years of my professional life. I was hired to read and write film scripts, but was later assigned run-of-the-mill television shows. I penned almost ten episodes a day, and, after a while, figured something was unsettling. The people were lovely, the job was all right, and I kept postponing the hard conversation to another day. On weekends, I would leave the city to teach visually impaired children with an NGO. We would leave Saturday night, arrive Sunday morning. I would conduct my workshops through the day and be back in office on Monday to artistically tell the world why papaya is a must-eat skincare fruit.

One day, while brainstorming for a digital platform, my bosses proposed turning my personal initiative, Project FUEL, into a show. This was a time when FUEL wasn't an organization but a one-man army. I was amused at the proposition but was sure that this work, to collect human wisdom, wasn't going to end up being a confrontational digital series. It was the mission of my life and larger than my own understanding. I told my bosses that this idea didn't belong there and neither did I. A few weeks later, I returned to a part-time job and started working towards shaping Project FUEL more thoughtfully to take it to places it deserved to go.

The feeling of belonging to someone or something isn't a safe one. In fact, it's quite nerve-racking. But it's assuring nonetheless. This buzz about a guiding intuition is valid when it comes to discovering where you belong.

I belong to house parties more than clubs. I belong to a smaller city surrounded by mountains with occasional trips to the metropolis. I belong to classrooms more than fancy award shows. I belong to communities more than diplomatic conferences. I belong to my parents' home and the tiny upcycled table in my office, on which I light my favourite incense sticks, overlooking a garden decked with green vines and seasonal flowers. I belong here and many more places I haven't arrived at yet. The search is a lifelong one. And therefore, messages such as the ones in the Instagram 'other messages' folder help to keep me motivated and enthusiastic.

No doubt, it's a hard question to ask and answer—do you belong? But it's harder to ignore the agony and uncertainty if you do not. Almost everyone is in pursuit of feeling like they belong. A small trick helps: If you can high-five yourself without feeling awkward or raising a few eyebrows, you may be in a good spot. How do you get there? I am not sure. But what I am sure about is that it feels like a place where you are most at peace, with yourself and within yourself.

## 37

What is the
worst thing that
could happen
to you?

The good thing is you just have to take a guess. It's a solidified assumption you are making on the basis of things that have happened previously or that you fear are going to happen. None of us can really pinpoint the exact details about our worst things (or 'thing', in case you won a mercy lottery from the world). Even if we do have an inclination about what it could be, we do not know when it will take place.

For the less fortunate ones, like me, one such moment has already passed. I will tell you all about it, but let me begin by saying it was embarrassing as hell for me and full of a lifetime of humour for others.

So the story begins in Sri Lanka, in a gorgeous old restored café called Sooriya Village. I was there with a creative tribe on a road trip, and we were painting a mural on the boundary wall of the café as part of a collaboration. It was a quaint, vintage bungalow with trees that spoke of its legacy. It had a small pond with golden-yellow fish and bright green patches of algae at the bottom. The woodwork along with the tapestry created a hard-to-forget vibe. After painting for a few hours in the sun, I stepped inside to sit under the shade of a tree in the garden. My eyes caught sight of a small yet charming mango tree bearing just two velvety green raw mangoes, the size of my palm. I looked around to ask one of the staff members what kind it was and if one could consume it. There was nobody around, so I resumed painting.

Later in the day, while taking a break, I was sipping some iced tea with a friend inside the café when I noticed a smartly dressed young woman walk out of the kitchen. As a reflex action, my memory of the mangoes resurfaced, and as she passed by our table, I asked her, 'Hey! Is plucking your mangoes allowed?' My friend, who was sitting across me, gasped for air. The girl rolled her eyes to the moon and back. My naive self was still unaware of the inappropriateness of the question. 'Excuse me! Do you know what you are talking about?' Unfazed, I responded, 'Yes! Of course. I am talking about your mangoes. Given that there are only two. I thought I'll ask for permission.' She could have fainted or got me arrested, if not for the owner, who knew I was a well-meaning guy. She walked away giving me the coldest stare of my life. To say that every customer in the café was looking at me strangely would be too much detail to share. However, even after all this, I had no clue what had agitated her so much. Then my friend explained to me that my question had seemed to be less about the garden and more about the anatomy of the woman.

My face turned red. My body wanted to curl into itself, and if you had squeezed me tight, I would have produced a bucket full of nervous sweat. I was so embarrassed. Sometimes, embarrassing things can be the worst stuff to happen to you. Like a friend of mine whose trackpants got stuck on a luggage conveyer belt so artistically that the pants and his boxers were down to his knees for a couple of seconds. The two seconds must have felt like a lifetime to him, I am sure. You can't prepare a crisis kit for something like that.

People have confessed to me that losing a parent is a hard 'worst thing' to make peace with. It will happen, some day, unknown, and this uncertainty builds up to that unfavourable truth. For singers, the worst thing could be losing their voice; for sportspersons, losing their physical fitness; for craftspeople, losing their imagination—these are easy conjectures to draw.

Our worst fears often find roots in the things we love most: relationships, skill sets, ideas, abilities that we derive joy from or construct our self-esteem with. And even though it seems nearly impossible to predict what the future holds in respect to them, taking into consideration our fears helps cultivate our gratitude towards each of these things. If you think the worst thing that could happen to you is the passing away of a loved one, then go out and spend time with them. If you feel your ability to write might get hampered over time, then discipline yourself to write something every day. If it's your health that you think might deteriorate (which will happen to all of us) then exercise a little so that old age doesn't attack all your joints and bolts.

The semi-delusional angel says, 'Never borrow from the future. If you worry about what may happen and it does not happen then you have worried in wane. Even if it does happen, you have to worry twice.' Look for the pragmatic angel that cautions you against asking a girl for two of her mangoes and saves you a groundbreaking boo-boo.

## 38

What do
you most need
encouragement
for?

While walking along the old boulevard in Baku, Azerbaijan, I saw a young boy, about four or five years old, calling out to his grandfather, who was sitting on a park bench nearby. 'Baba . . . Baba,' he said repeatedly. The old man looked up from the newspaper he was reading. As soon as the young boy had his attention, he ran across the cobbled path with his arms wide open, smashed into a big green bush and exclaimed, 'It hugs me back. Did you see? This bush hugs me back.' The grandfather, probably engrossed in worldly affairs, putting aside his wisdom, smiled and nodded in agreement. 'It does. How lovely!' he responded. Encouraged, the boy ran back over and over into the bush. The grandfather acted surprised and cheered him on every single time.

It was one of the most joyous things I had witnessed in a while.

I need encouragement to be this innocent. Wide-eyed about the simplest pleasures of life and not afraid of running into a bush in a public park. There is a long list of people who need some nudging to come along on a similar quest. People who are consumed in self-pity or suffering from the disease of busyness.

Vibhor Yadav, a close friend and a genius photographer, takes pictures that make me cry with all kinds of good feelings. Early on in our friendship, we discovered that we loved to collaborate, had mutual respect for each other's talent and an unrivalled desire to serve the world. Giving this bond a concrete shape, together we started an Instagram handle called 'Unposted Postcards'. The process is really simple: People send us a request with a name and a theme; I write the text, Vibhor finds a relevant representational photo, and we address a postcard to a stranger on the web to bring a smile to their face. We post one every day. The reason I bring this up is because 80 per cent of the requests are themed around encouragement. Either urging an old friend to reconnect or a partner to slow down and not be in a constant rush or asking to love oneself despite one's flaws.

Take, for instance, the request a wife sent for her husband who she said was loved by many. But he refused to relax and worked all the time. She wanted us to write a postcard asking him to calm down and persuade him to not be so overdriven.

So we made one. It read:

Dear Anant,

When I married you, time moved as slow as the moon on a starry night. And now it skips to the next thing like a YouTube ad. Won't it be nice to sometimes stop and over boil the milk because we were so busy talking, stare at the face of children and lose track of time, stroll gently across cafes on our streets and chat about silly things? I would like you to know that you are loved and that you don't have to prove anything to anyone. Just remember to schedule yourself in your to-do list and perhaps for a

fleeting moment we could be the most memorable act in this circus of life.
Let's spend a lifetime,
In a single moment someday.

The series of postcards is an effort to remind people that no matter what you are going through, there is always help around. What we have to say is not something that is new or has never been said before. But it must be said so that our words of encouragement can act as alarm clocks for those who need a little poke, a tap on the shoulder or a long, warm hug to be prompted towards the meaningful stuff.

I like the word 'encouragement' a lot. It originates from two French words, 'en' meaning 'in' and 'corage' meaning 'courage'. 'In courage'—the hope is for people to find that extra push to accept who they are or to pause on their way home to notice the moon or to call someone they care about to express how they feel.

What is the one thing you need the most encouragement for?

## 39

If you were handed
an envelope with the
date of your death
inside, and you
knew you could do
nothing to alter
your fate,
would you
look?

I came across this question in an inspiring book by the biophysicist and bestselling author Gregory Stock. As soon as I read it, I paused and thought, would I look?

Many people over the years have paused very much like me over this question. Primarily because in the simple choice of finding out or avoiding the answer, a great deal is revealed about us as people. Those who are okay finding out say that it will help them make the most of their remaining days and not take anything for granted. They will value every single moment, relationship and idea they hold close. But I wonder what it is about death that heightens this sense of gratitude. Is it an eventual loss that we want to win over by living the most in the time we have? Or is it to approach life with a conscious understanding of how far we have come and to rise above the uncertainty of how far we will go? But shouldn't we already be doing our best to make the most of life irrespective of the countdown to death?

There is a second school of thought about this question as well. Many people say they wouldn't want to know the expiry date of their life because that information would take away their joy and peace. If you know how many days you have left on the calendar, you will pass them cognizant of the fact that the end is near. And not everyone is okay with that news.

One person went to the extreme of saying, 'To know when you will die is to die a little every day up until the exact date.' But don't we already know that death is the inevitable truth of existence? What has come must return to its elements one day. How does putting a date on it help avoid its factuality?

I think what Gregory Stock hints at, with this question, is having a subtle sense of control over death. Whether we like the power of that control or not is subjective but the curiosity to explore it lies within all of us. It also brings forth many other perspectives on how we have lived so far. Have we expressed enough love to our partners, taken the risk in our careers that we have been postponing for a while, will we finally find time for the book we have procrastinated to read or write, will health now be a priority or does it not matter any more?

Holy books and saints have for generations preached about the finiteness of life. To accept that no new day is promised. The exit might take place in the next second or fifty years later. But that shouldn't alter your lifestyle. I want to raise my hand and say to these spiritual leaders that they are right but it's tough to practise. And perhaps I know their response, 'That is why not everyone became enlightened like the Buddha but has a chance to.'

For some of us, I am afraid, the enlightenment is on hold. We are still caught up in the heartbreak of being dumped and awaiting a reply to a text, figuring out if applying sandalwood paste every evening will make our skin glow, or if we will ever make it to a Rihanna concert. These are important questions, and I wouldn't want to die without knowing the answers.

Death, arguably, is a topic of universal interest. A microscope of some sort, making us the deciding body on how much we want to zoom into particular components of our lives.

It's a reality check for some and a denied truth for others. All I know is that when we do arrive at the final checkpost of life, it would be wonderful to have enjoyed the journey. In the salvation home in Varanasi, speaking to the residents in their last days, I learnt that one way to enjoy the journey is to find beauty in simple things. Mukti Bhavan played soulful bhajans and devotional songs three times a day. 'Some people,' the manager, Mr Shukla, told me, 'stop and admire a note or the sound of the instruments as if they have never heard it before, even if they have. They pause to appreciate it and find beauty in it.' But that's not true of everyone, he added. 'People who are too critical or too proud are the ones who find it hard to find joy in small things because their minds are preoccupied with "seemingly" more important things.'

The phrase from the poet John Donne's writing, 'For whom the bell tolls', is a metaphoric probe. Back in the day, when someone passed away, the church would toll the bell to apprise everyone in town that the person was no more. The people would ask, 'For whom does the bell toll?' John Donne, through his work, responds to the question by saying, 'It tolls for thee.' Meaning that the death of another human being is a reminder that our time here is limited. He writes, 'Any man's death diminishes me, and therefore never send to know for whom the bells tolls; it tolls for thee.'

If we are to be told the 'when' about our death, the obvious next question is 'how'? To arrive at an adequate answer, it might be worth exploring if death is a success or a failure. Because as my friend Caspian puts it, 'One day we're all going to die, all of the other days we aren't.'

## 40

On a scale of
1 to 10, how much
have you loved
people and
yourself?

I met Arno Michaelis at the World Youth Conference for Kindness in New Delhi. At first glance, he looked like an American rock star. Covered in tattoos, with a scruffy beard and a warm aura that was welcoming and comforting. But the comforting aura had been long in the making, a journey of many years.

During the course of our interaction, I found out that Arno was a former White supremacist. He said he was a reverend of the self-declared 'Racial Holy War', a belief which popularized the notion that White people should unite and start a holy war against Jews and other minorities. Arno was also the lead singer of the hate-metal band Centurion. He became a White supremacist when he was seventeen and helped found Northern Hammerskins, one of the largest skinhead organizations in the world.

It has been nine years since he left the skinhead community. Rising above his hateful actions of the past, he is now a public speaker, author and director of Serve 2 Unite, an organization he founded with Pardeep Kaleka in 2012 after Wade Michael Page, a White supremacist, murdered six people, including Kaleka's father, in a Wisconsin Sikh temple.

From a past rooted in violence to endorsing peace, non-violence and compassion across world communities, Arno has come a long way in learning lessons on loving others and oneself.

Mesmerized by his story and tattoos, I asked him what made him quit a movement that he vouched to give his life for. Without a pause, with a big smile, he said, 'I was tired. Because hate is exhausting. Love is so much more effortless.' Those words made the hair on my arms stand up on end. It was such a simple statement yet pregnant with meaning. He added he was friends with the same people today he had once loathed. Even when they made him feel cared for earlier, he had not accepted it. And now he wanted to give back to the world.

In his story, there is a reflection of all of us. I often wonder that in the times we live in, do people really have acceptance for receiving and giving unexpected love. And how does one acknowledge it when someone does show that they care about you?

John Patrick Goggins, in a play called *The Curious Savage* wrote a beautiful dialogue which to me is one of the greatest lessons ever to be practised. He said, 'People say I love you all the time—when they say, "Take an umbrella, it's raining", or "Hurry back" or even "Watch out, you'll break your neck". There are hundreds of ways of wording it—you just have to listen for it, my dear.'

It is so imperative to pay attention to these small gestures, unconventional yet significant ways of compassion and romance. Because they are present in abundance and handed over to us almost every day, whether or not we are looking for them or celebrating their existence. A friend of mine in college once said to me, complaining, 'My parents don't really care about my life.' When I asked why, he said, 'They have the same set of questions to ask on every call: How was your day? Did you eat?' I sort of laughed, because I know this for sure, that if we are waiting for the exact words 'I love you' to be spoken then we might be waiting hopelessly for someone to speak in a language we understand, but ignoring the love language they are comfortable in. People often express in instalments, in capsules, in hints. It doesn't mean they don't care, it just means we did not know that there were different ways to word it.

Noticing the smallest of changes, recognizing little acts of doing, complimenting when it's least expected and having enough courage to voice something positive are all reminders that you matter. You belong. You are treasured.

'Let me drive you home.'

'It reminded me of you.'

'Come here. Let me fix it.'

'Do you want to grab a coffee?'

'Thank God you called.'

'You have such a long life.'

'I saved a piece for you.'

'I wish you were here.'

'Take my seat.'

'Have a good day.'

'Don't buy it. Take mine.'

'I made your favourite—.'

'Text me when you get home.'

'Are you hungry?'

I share this laundry list so that you can gauge a better number on the scale of how much you have loved people in your own way.

The other thought that kept me awake that night after my conversation with Arno was how he was able to love himself for what he did and truly align with a new life. That takes bravery and a gallon of forgiveness for the self. I applaud him for it. Most people I ask the question, 'On a scale of 1 to 10 how much have you loved yourself?', respond with a number below five on average. We chant our failures so much or project our expectations so high that there is little room left for embracing our own self.

To add to that pressure is the scrutiny of social media. I know scrolling and tapping through your social media feed might make it seem like everyone's life is amazing. Better than yours. People are travelling the best of locations, brewing incredible collaborations, looking their best, trying out new cuisines. The truth is your life is equally amazing. You too have food to eat, friends to call, home to be. Just because you are not putting it out on Instagram doesn't mean that it doesn't exist or that it's not worthy. The sun is not biased with how many followers you have. Water still quenches the thirst of those whose posts have no likes. Relax. Enjoy. Don't weigh your worth on someone else's balance beam.

What problem
of yours would
you like to solve?

If we are attempting to answer this one, then let me pull out my encyclopaedia of problems. The list is so long I can easily put you to sleep until 2080. Why does my maid take so many holidays? Can flight temperatures be regulated personally so that you don't disembark feeling like an ice cube leaving an igloo? Taxes. My curd and chips addiction. From fitness to relationships, from jobs to hobbies, from personal to professional issues, the struggles of modern life are never-ending. But ignoring a problem isn't solving it. The best way to find its resolution is to acknowledge its effect on our psyche and course-correct to a desired routine.

Let me confess a problem I took the longest road to resolving. I had major trust issues with people after having been betrayed a few times. I was dejected about how someone could use me for their own good and later turn it around as per their convenience. The twisted experiences during college had left me sore about opening myself up to others to a degree where uninhibited trust could flow. I would feel the urge of wanting to make others feel worthy of this but a voice in my head would caution me repeatedly.

On my first solo trip to the picturesque town of Kalimpong, I met a monk in the foothills of a monastery I was strolling by. I sat across him and posed my worldly questions, one of which was: 'Should I trust again if my trust has been broken repeatedly?' He thought for a moment and replied, 'Well, you must to be like the sun.' 'What does that mean?' I asked. And he explained, 'On some days you go sunbathing, stretch out and soak in all the sunshine in the world. And on others, you put on your shades, roll up your windows, draw your curtains and curse the hell out of the sun. The sun doesn't change because of how you behave. It shows up every day just like it used to. Try to be like the sun.'

I got my answer. It is easy to not trust any more if your capacity to love has been questioned. But I have a strong sense that to be able to love or trust or care despite all the hurt is a powerful act of living, uninhibited by the confusion and complexities of what you mean to people. Aware of the fact that you won't be hardened by hard knocks. Better informed! But not rigid and rogue. Your virtues don't have to hang their heads in shame and feel guilty.

Sometime back, I chanced upon a brilliant post by author Elizabeth Gilbert on her Instagram page. She wrote:

> Mooji tells the story of a young man whom he'd once worked with, who couldn't focus on his meditation and spiritual practice because he was in such distress over a romantic relationship that had just ended. The young man's mind was too troubled by problems, he claimed, to be able to seek inner peace. Mooji asked the young man, 'But what was your biggest problem three problems ago?'
>
> I started laughing when I heard this. I immediately got the wisdom of the question, and saw how it's true in my own life. Whatever is bothering me today seems so terribly urgent, even impossible, to solve. But if you

asked me what my biggest problem was 'three problems ago', it was something else entirely. Something that has now resolved itself. Something that I thought would never fix, something that I thought needed my constant worry and anxiety, something that I thought would haunt me forever . . . and yet now it's gone. If you had told me three problems ago that I didn't need to worry so much because everything would ultimately be all right, I would've told you to go to hell. I would've told you that the problem needed and deserved my complete anxious attention. And yet, when I think about my old resolved problems, I'm not sure that it *was* my constant anxious attention that solved them. Something solved them, to be sure. When the critical moment came, I knew what to do. Or somebody else did. Or it all blew up, or it was a nightmare, yet here we are. One way or another, it ended. My biggest problems from thirty years ago are long gone. My biggest problem from twenty years ago is a dim memory. As for my biggest problem three problems ago? I can barely remember what it was. And yet, when I think about the biggest problem I am facing right now, I still believe that it needs my anxiety in order to be solved. But what if I have faith that—three problems from now—this one will be solved too? Then I can relax into the mystery and feel held.

I secretly nodded in agreement when I read this. When I contemplate the depth of it, the question morphs into, 'What was your heart-breaking, insanely imperative issue three heart-breaking, insanely imperative issues ago?' The concerns that annihilate our peace of mind seem like they will swallow us, but somehow we survive. We wake up to a new day, picking up the battle all over again, sometimes willingly, sometimes hesitantly. Despite the problem at hand, we all hold the possibility to bloom again like old dreams and trimmed branches.

Which emotion
do you hide
the most from
the world?

In every human heart, there is a backbencher emotion. One that doesn't want to be seen, pointed out or confronted. It likes to illustrate the trouble behind the back of other happy emotions; the ones that get all the praise and recognition. Public spotlight for it is an occasion of mass embarrassment.

In your heart, what would you say is that backbencher emotion? Lust? Rage? Arrogance? Love? Fear? Loneliness? Happiness? Craziness? Considerateness? Ignorance? Grief? Anxiety? Sarcasm? Anything else?

Some of us become experts at bottling up that one emotion we think makes us look ugly. Our ability to supress it may stem from knowing people wouldn't receive it well, or a societal bias that considers it an outright negative one, or backed by a personal philosophy, or out of peer pressure, assuming it will ruin your brand image.

Take, for instance, crying. Men are told from childhood that it's an unmanly thing to do. That they have to learn how to hide sadness than show it. Many men trade balling their eyes out with punching the wall or breaking something. For women, it's about being polite and graceful. Showing their 'crazy' side would be considered inappropriate and vulgar in some cultures, so they gobble up loud laughter even when they want to literally roll on the floor laughing.

This hiding can be a personal choice as well. To show the world my disappointed side is very hard for me. Nobody made me sign a contract to have a perpetual smiling face, but it's still a challenge. I am someone who likes to believe in people, but that doesn't mean I am never let down or have my hopes dashed. I find it hard to expose how dejected I am with a situation or someone's behaviour to a situation because of an inner voice. I avoid listening to it as much as I can. And to tell you the truth, I have become good at covering up my dejectedness. The stereotype of wanting to be seen happy initiated this, but over time, it has been propagated by a fear of not being accepted in any other light. Therefore, I practise showing my unveiled disappointment in a trusted circle, in the company of family, friends and colleagues I have known for a while. They don't mind me being silly or throwing a tantrum as a result of being disgruntled.

If I overanalyse and rant for a minute here, I can tell you most of my disappointment gets activated when people say one thing and do another. Or when someone believes in another person but doesn't factor in a single ounce of personal motivation in their own self. And most certainly when people miss deadlines. Just because I am a rain lover doesn't necessarily mean I will be happy getting drenched in December when it was supposed to pour in June.

Fear can be paralysing if you do not acknowledge all the times you were able to survive it. Anxiety, if concealed for a long period, can lead to clinical depression. Happiness, if not demonstrated in the most comfortable way, might transform into a half-lived regret. Unconfessed arrogance might take the shape of verbal abuse or an ego trap. We all are aware of the repercussions and have gathered enough evidence about that one emotion that always gets the better of us.

I know it will take some time until I train myself to mouth my disappointment. Till then, I would like to subscribe to what Dr Brené Brown, who studies vulnerability, courage, authenticity and shame, highlights from her research. The humiliation of rejection and seeing vulnerability as a weakness is what corrupts our story and tires out our conscience. She writes in her book, *Daring Greatly*, 'Vulnerability isn't good or bad. It's not what we call a dark emotion, nor is it always a light, positive experience. Vulnerability is the core of all emotions and feelings. To feel is to be vulnerable. To believe vulnerability is weakness is to believe that feeling is weakness.' Almost in a consoling fashion, she explains, 'When I look at narcissism through the vulnerability lens, I see the shame-based fear of being ordinary. I see the fear of never feeling extraordinary enough to be noticed, to be lovable, to belong, or to cultivate a sense of purpose.'

Maybe some day the backbencher emotions will also see their value and shy away from raising their hand. Not labelled for being mischievous and dismissed for affecting the decorum. But organically recognized for their presence.

When I do approach that sweet spot where I can flash my hiding emotion—disappointment—with ease, I will put a massive billboard on the entrance for everyone else who is on their way to this point. It would have an anonymous quote I love: 'Frankly, there isn't anyone you couldn't learn to love once you've heard their story.'

## 43

What should have changed you but did not and what shouldn't have but did?

Criticism should have altered my determination but somehow it did not succeed. Sceptics of my enthusiasm couldn't chip off my sense of grit to show up consistently in classrooms and teach. Despite the fact that I looked too young to dip my toes into a subject as serious or consequential as 'human wisdom'. When at seventeen you start passing on life lessons, and nearly no one is ready to lend you some credibility, it's bound to crush you a tad, or, let me be honest, a massive amount. I was affected by their comments, but not to the point where I would abandon something I dearly believed in. Years later, it remains a mission that thrives on the emotional, social and financial contribution of so many people. That's my answer to the first part of the question.

Regarding what shouldn't have changed me but did, I would have to say it's the plants in my back garden. Each plant is a progress of my patience report. Earlier, I mostly wanted things to happen at lightning speed, but now I keep a margin to let things take their time. Plants really shouldn't have changed me, but I would be lying if I didn't admit that they did, deeply. They taught me to live life in slow motion, just like they do. If you inspect them every day, it seems as if nothing is happening. But if you stop hovering over them every second, the growth does show. Now, whenever I am in a panic about something, I head to my garden, walk through the plants and observe them in silence for a while. A masterclass unfolds.

I am cognizant that some hard knocks life throws at us do hold the power to change us, for better or worse. But we do have a say in it. The story of Hadi validates that for me.

On a ninety-day tour in 2016, where I was documenting the life lessons of refugees, I met this twenty-seven-year-old sharp, jovial and stylish man in Germany. He shared his life lesson, 'Be happy no matter what happens.' To detail his learning, he told me, 'Before I took that boat to flee from Syria during the war, through the sea route, I used to watch videos of other people doing the same on YouTube. I used to tell myself, "Oh, that is so dangerous. I would never do that." But then I had to take the same option as I had no other choice.'

He added, 'You know, it might sound crazy but when I was in the boat fleeing with forty-four other people, we were singing. I really enjoyed that experience. I was mesmerized that we were in the middle of an ocean. No one in sight—as far as one could see. And there we were, a bunch of people in a boat, singing. I learnt from them to enjoy the moment even if it was the hardest. Don't you love yourself when you are happy? Who doesn't? Happiness guides you to better things.'

He even wore his sunglasses all through his journey. And when the boat arrived in Greece, his friend told him, 'Hadi, take the glasses off, you are a refugee.' But he kept them on because he wanted people to know he was a person with dreams, desires and style, not an alien descending from another planet. He chose to retain what made him happy. It did not reduce his challenges but certainly helped strengthen his attitude when confronted with the worst—rebuilding a life in another country

In the hopscotch of your answers, I would like to sneak in a gentle reminder. Irrespective of what you discover, consider this: This is the first draft of our being. Occasional appreciation, constant creation and timely editing keeps it tight and relevant. The text is often punctuated too much—to please, to honour, to forgive, to let go, to give in, to conform, to rebel, to think, to think no more, to flow, to observe, to condense, to expatiate. As long as the subtext is safe, it seems all is well. A bunch of arresting memories appear to be a persistent craving. Apart from that, there are some misinformed anecdotes, some misfit words, misinterpreted conversations, misled dreams and miscalculated risks.

But then, in a long passage of time, through the tunnel of emotions, our being urges the reader to bear in mind—this is the first draft.

## 44

What
happened
to you?

For this one, you are on your own. I won't be offering any insight, anecdote or personal reference to assist you. Why? I would love for you to define the boundaries of your answer without having to do so within any context or limitation. Even when I play out this exercise with people in person, I usually leave them to assimilate what it means to them.

Meanwhile, because we have space and time to fill, let me share an absolutely non-related yet heart-warming story I love.

It is about Franz Kafka, the Bohemian novelist and short-story writer, celebrated for his soulful contribution to twentieth-century literature.

Kafka, during his last trip to Berlin, the story goes, came across a little girl in the Steglitzer park where he would go for regular walks. The girl was desolate, sobbing profusely as she had lost her beloved doll.

Moved by her tears, Kafka came up with a solution to help her look for the doll, and requested the girl to meet him the next day at the same spot.

He returned with a letter from the doll, compassionately explaining the reason for her absence. He read it to the little girl when they met. 'Please do not mourn me, I have gone on

a trip to see the world. I will write to you of my adventures.'
For several weeks, he continued to write letters on behalf
of the doll, consoling the girl and notifying her of the doll's
imagined travel adventures. His heartfelt letters brought
assurances to the little girl.

After his tuberculosis worsened, Kafka decided to return
to Prague—where he would die a year later—but decided
to meet the girl one last time, presenting her with a doll.
The new doll looked different from the original one. The
difference was explained in an attached letter that read, 'My
travels have changed me.'

I was so touched by this story that I dug up more on it
online. I found a comforting addition to the already beautiful
story. The write-up on the book said, 'Many years later, the
now grown girl found a letter stuffed into an unnoticed crevice
in the cherished replacement doll.'

In summary, it said: 'Everything that you love, you
will eventually lose, but in the end, love will return in a
different form.'

## 45

What is your
recipe to deal
with silence?

A friend of mine left for a short Vipassana course. She proclaimed the ten-day retreat was a detoxification of the body and mind. She would eat organic food, sleep on time and—the most insane part—not speak for ten days. Now, since I have known her for a long time, I knew the last part would be a bit of a stretch for her. But she was convinced she would be able to do it.

Five days later, I got a call from her that she had left the programme midway because she couldn't take the silence. It made her uncomfortable to a level where she started feeling anxious.

I know this is not only her truth but is shared by a large number of people. We don't often pause to evaluate how comfortable we are with silence. In olden times, it would have been easier to handle. I remember noticing my grandparents and other people in my maternal village working for hours with no communication. You can say they were absorbed in the activity and therefore needed no other distraction. But even outside working hours, I saw my grandmother remain quiet for long durations without feeling awkward or anxious.

Today, the quiet time has been replaced by the act of scrolling. As soon as we find a moment of solace, our hand, with some magnetic force, reaches for the cell phone.

The thumb starts to scroll in a scholarly fashion. To kill time, we take refuge in the outpouring of information available to us at a click. But there is a bigger question at play. What are we escaping from, have we even fully experienced a moment of quietude? Have we consciously allowed ourselves to be in its presence without apprehensions and frivolous distractions?

During meditation, more than the passing thoughts, it's the pursuit of silence that makes people lifelong learners of the practice. Our brains seem to be wired to constantly think and use sound as a toy. Silence outlines the noise. It provides us a moment of pause.

Many people pick up a book, listen to music or daydream. There is no wrong or right suggestion you can take up for hints on how to fill your silent space. But there is a definite need for each of us to craft our own recipes to deal with silence. In my lectures, in mid-sentence, I sometimes pause and fall silent. I am neither projecting anger nor highlighting frustration or exhaustion. I am just soaking in the classroom, its people, its ambience, and how it makes me feel. But the students often get perturbed and ask if everything is all right. If they have made a mistake. If something has offended me. No one, at first, seems willing to enjoy the unexpected silence with me. When I don't give in to their demands of reasoning with my quietness, they begin to participate. And collectively, we create a space where we can be together but don't have to actively eliminate sounds to avoid the damage of their absence.

Of course, my interpretation is limited to my experience. There are many shades of silence. It's not a dish but a buffet. Poet and psychotherapist Paul Goodman, better known as a social critic and anarchist philosopher, investigates nine kinds of silence.

There is the dumb silence of slumber or apathy; the sober silence that goes with a solemn animal face; the fertile silence of awareness, pasturing the soul, whence emerge new thoughts; the alive silence of alert perception, ready to say, 'This . . . this . . .'; the musical silence that accompanies absorbed activity; the silence of listening to another speak, catching the drift and helping him be clear; the noisy silence of resentment and self-recrimination, loud and subvocal speech but sullen to say it; baffled silence; the silence of peaceful accord with other persons or communion with the cosmos.

In moments of awe, it's easier to be speechless. During beautiful sunsets, long walks on a beach, road trips in the mountains, and in prayer rooms—it's easier to find calm and be mindful of it. The trick is to bring the resounding effect of that experience to our routine. To consciously allow silence to permeate into our schedules. So that we don't have to make small talk, watch unnecessary Internet junk or scroll endlessly, but rather enjoy in its unfolding peace, the luxury of boredom or the adventures of daydreaming.

You can choose to answer the question in reference to silence in the inner or the outer world. The prophecy of Nobel Prize–winning bacteriologist Robert Koch in 1905 might not be far off as he cautions, 'The day will come when man will have to fight noise as inexorably as cholera and the plague.'

## 46

What do you
need to
unlearn?

Interrupting others. Taking things personally. Scrolling. Pleasing everyone. Having rice for dinner every day. Over-thinking. Snapping at parents for no reason. Assuming. Over-promising. Fretting over jet lag. Writing long emails. Saying sorry as a reflex action for expressing yourself. The list goes on.

I can write a whole book on this subject. Merely because I have witnessed, first-hand, grave ramifications of the single act of learning half-baked truths or false biases. During my travel in rural villages or marginalized communities across the world, most of the time the response to the question, 'What has life taught you?' is met with a dismissive, 'I don't know the answer because I did not go to school.' People confuse being literate with being educated. Nothing could be more misleading. We all have met people who, despite having three degrees to show off, lack basic courtesy and politeness. Five minutes into a conversation with them, you would have rolled your eyes fifty times. I have so much sympathy for them that I would like to help them claim a refund for their academic qualifications. Then there are those who can't read a single letter or sign their name, yet are so hospitable and respectful that you couldn't care less if they know how much is four multiplied by four.

During these community visits, I invest a considerable chunk of time assisting villagers, especially women who married young, and later come to the realization that knowledge and wisdom are not something one picks up only within the structure of formal education. Relationships with nature, the community, children, family and cattle are all a source of learning. Of course, they know it subconsciously, but do not dare to admit it.

Just because we have known a bit of information long enough, we might deem it valuable and feel defiance towards unlearning it. A genius exercise designed by one of our Project FUEL fellows, Jaideep Joshi, illustrates this best. In the workshop, Jaideep begins by asking participants to draw an apple on a sheet of paper. Once the drawing is finished, he requests us to take one hard look at our apple, instructing us further to exchange our drawing with the person sitting next to us. As we hold the work of our partner in our hands, he tells us to compare our apple with the apple we are now looking at, and list three comparisons between the two.

As the activity concludes, he makes us stand and read our responses one by one. You wouldn't believe it, but people write things like: 'My apple was smaller than his.' or 'There was a leaf on my apple, but it is missing from this one.' Jaideep communicates that we have been conditioned to believe a comparison means pointing out differences, and our obvious automatic response is to point out things that are unlike rather than alike.

He is correct in his analysis. I have done this activity with hundreds of people in almost five countries. When asked to compare two things or more, most adults pen down the dissemblance. But children up to the age of thirteen or fourteen always highlight the semblance. Won't this make for a great behavioural study as to at what age we start believing in these complicated notions of learning?

American writer and futurist Alvin Toffler once wrote, 'The illiterate of the twenty-first century will not be those who cannot read and write, but those who cannot learn, unlearn and relearn.'

Some concepts are so compellingly marketed to us over centuries that it seems almost foolish to not buy into them. Take, for instance, the importance of money and the endless chase to acquire it. Our media, society and culture pays notorious significance to earning money, often making it look like the goal rather than a means to achieving something. Instead of learning how to use it as a vehicle, we end up giving it the driver's seat, losing all control and direction in moulding our lifestyle and relationships.

My mentor and friend Akshay Cherian, during a masterclass, shared a perspective that I had lived but never condensed in that manner. He said he was taught, 'Everybody is rich. Just that some people have money.' Think about it, isn't the realization of that statement mind-blowing? Akshay made us learn that money is only one form of currency but there are several other currencies that exist. Our ideas, experiences, skills are also currencies with merit. He made us unlearn that money was the prerequisite to feeling empowered.

If you think about it, we can spend another lifetime unlearning the things we have learnt till now. But we can begin today by first admitting to what information, behaviour trait or belief system colours our thoughts and then follow it up with corrective actions. Writer J.R. Rim wrote beautifully: 'Intelligence is what we learn. Wisdom is what we unlearn.'

I doubt any person, with some practical introspection, would deny the fact that the only way we can add more is by deleting something. Maybe the problem isn't that we don't know anything. Maybe there is a fear that we know a lot. We are not looking for people who can help us learn, but rather those who can help us unlearn.

## 47

In the world
where everyone
is selling something,
what do you want
to buy?

I turned to my communications manager, Mehak, to get a direction for this question. The same way she effortlessly helps me plan my schedule and travel and documents and life, she responded with a smile, 'Well, people mostly have the power to give tangible things. I have a feeling what we want to buy is always intangible. I would encourage you to answer keeping that context in mind.'

She nudged me just enough to admit that it is true. Materialistic things—a fancy car, branded shoes, a summer home—might be our first thought about what we desire. But if we dig a little deeper, what we would like to buy is probably improving a relationship that doesn't value us as much as we would like, earning respect in a group of peers who constantly look down upon you, recognition for balancing home and work, or spending more time with loved ones instead of travelling far to earn your bread and butter.

While we are at this, I definitely would like to buy some time if I could. To read all the books on my to-do list. In fact, I would tug at the sleeves of business meetings, conferences and unnecessary commitments to let me swipe a card to sit at a bookstore for as long as I please.

If you think about it, the best place to invoke or sustain your sense of wonder is a bookstore. Shelf after shelf of awakened human beings condensed into thin sheets, embossed with ink and cemented by a thick spine. Their loose ends put together with tree glue and layered with covers of all shapes and sizes.

At first, a bookstore reeks of vulnerability, but if one hangs around a little longer, it's hard to miss the incense of humour, love and hard work. Each book is a reminder of the simple fact: No matter what each of those people thought about their day or the world at large thought of them, they were inspired to create. They drew inspiration from their daily routine and summoned self-belief to word their thoughts into emotions, emotions into words, words into sentences, paragraphs, a page, pages and finally a book.

A bookstore is a place of possibilities. A sum total of reflections of glorious folk tales, personal memoirs, painful historic wars, romances, playful poetry and all dreams that are fragile but still important. Therefore, they are still safe on wooden planks, with rusty glass windows as their guardian.

The most secular place in the world has to be a bookstore. Irrespective of being polar opposites in the real world, for their opinions to find an audience, people have to agree to stand beside each other at a bookstore. No matter how contemporary the subject, it will take pride in being housed in an old-fashioned, stone-layered bookstore. All religions conform to live in harmony only in two places: in God's heart and at a bookstore. Staunch Hindu ideologies don't sniffle at Islamic preaching there, Jewish proverbs don't disregard Buddhist wisdom, the learnings of Sufism are in tune with Christian hymns.

And perhaps that is why when dust gathers on them, they don't shrug it off or sneeze uncontrollably, their eyes welling and their backs strained. Rather, they hold space for the dust too, aware that humanity, fighting in their names, has forgotten to read their meaning and perhaps will return some day.

Bookstores are old leaves pressed between the relics of time, only to be discovered with nostalgia, tasted with humility and soaked in with the bliss of serendipity.

I think I have over-explained myself here. But that's okay, I suppose. It's time I am out to buy anyway.

## 48

If now was forever, would it be enough?

Some days, I leave my work chair at lunchtime and sit across the table, on the other side. As I nibble on a delicious home-cooked delicacy made by my mother, I notice my office room from the perspective of those who sit across me. Wow! I built this! This is my den. I get to come here and work. It's crazy how one small inquiry into people's life lessons has ushered me this far.

I wonder what it takes to create a life of fulfilment. Passion? Maybe. But not completely. One has to be a certain kind of crazy to make things happen even when the winds are against the motion. Crazy with creativity and consistency seems like a good mantra for tasting the thick and nourishing honey of contentment.

I do wish for every creative wizard in the world to build their own monastery. A place where the pressure of the world is lifted off your shoulders, where the walls testify to your presence, and the plants greet you with new flowers every week. A place where forgiveness comes easy and the mind is willing to lose the map.

In my case, if this moment was forever, it might not be enough. I am not even half done here. I am certainly en route, but not fully there yet. I wish to offer much more. Serve the world with my stories, talents, tales and kindness.

Also, silly jokes and stupidity. I haven't even seen the Northern Lights. I need a little longer to shape something I can call my forever. To celebrate those who have paved the way.

And if your answer was 'yes', this time that is passing is the best. It can be capsuled and labelled forever. Then here's my request: Pay it forward. Pay it backward. When you start to make it, ensure you recognize, reconcile and rejoice with people who helped you get here. They might have forgotten or stopped expecting it, but you shouldn't. Let people label it as your generosity, but you know that it is much more. It helps close the loop of success for you. It's unimportant how much you have; be willing to share. Play fair. It might not happen the same way for you. But that's okay. When you get to the position of having your piece of the pie, try to divide it into smaller bites for those who have craved it as much for you as you have. That will measure up to decorate your life meaningfully. Your success with what you have will be more satisfying. Your legacy will be more lasting. You don't have to do it because you will be rewarded for it. Do it because this phase that feels like forever is the accomplishment. Pay it forward, backward, upwards, downwards and in more ways that your mind can comprehend.

You are privileged if you have people around you who are genuinely happy for you. Not a sly agenda, not a hint of expectation, not an ulterior motive of wanting to be compensated. Just happy that you have opened up to the potential of your best life, and they wouldn't miss a moment to cheer you on.

Ah! That sounds like a good way to stamp forever on to a moment. For the rest of us who are in transit, offer words of encouragement, drop a prayer in the wish pond of the world, and when we do ask for help, stretch your arm and pull us up.

The view must be stunning from that moment. I can tell.

## 49

So far, in the gallery
of your life, are
you the art, the
artist or the
visitor?

My parents, I recall, had an unusual way of making our birthdays memorable. They would club buying anything important for the house with my sister's and my birthday. That meant it would arrive as a gift in the house to make the day special for us. I now look back at this technique as genius parenting. Not only did it give us children an opportunity to feel important, appreciated and awed by the size of the present, but also filled the gap of a particular necessity in the house.

I remember being eight years old and a colour television arriving home. *Tom and Jerry* played on the screen, my friends circled it, eating cake, and I was moved with the experience of it all. My sister got a centre table. The year after, it was a cupboard. A fridge. A new bed. A small stool. A new dinner set.

Boundless is the significance of that characteristic of innovation in a middle-class family like ours. My parents had limited means, and yet they were able to use them intelligently to bring comfort for us both as tangible resources as well as emotional supplement. I think, in the gallery of life, I call them artists.

With my loud mouth and dramatic enthusiasm, I wouldn't call myself a visitor for sure. I am juggling between the art and the artist. I think I will go with being the art. I feel this way because even if I subtract all my talents, my indecisive attitude while shopping and my superpower of driving my mom nuts with my procrastination, I would still consider myself interesting. Someone worth sitting down with, talking to and having a good time. I am art that engages, doesn't matter whether in a comforting or a disturbing way, in a confusing or a clear manner. The purpose of art is to grab your attention and try to hold it for as long as possible. Certain pieces will grab you by the collar and push you back, while others will sneak into your mind and follow you home.

When the drumrolls have died, the applause has slipped into oblivion, when the hooting has settled into stillness, when the crowd has cleared the room, when the flashes have faded away, when the praise has perished, when a hush takes over the hype, I will still refer to myself as art. Where being grateful comes to me as naturally as breathing. Where my mindfulness liberates my fears, where I belong to no one but myself. That, my folks, is another stage to stand upon. On it, another kind of spotlight envelops our existence, another genre of music echoes in all dimensions. Life sits in the audience and awaits our act. I am trying to give my best performance. Shining in the crowd, glowing in the solitude.

At some point in our lives, we will be all three: the art, the artist and the visitor. The question invites you to think of the role you enjoy the most and would like to return to as much as possible. If you are the art, what contributes to the masterpiece? If it's the artist, what is your evidence? If you are a visitor, what have you enjoyed in this role?

Whatever be the answer, I am happy and relieved that we are all in this gallery together.

What is
your life
lesson?

There is a wide smile on my face as I ask this question. For you, it might be the last question in the journey of reading this book. For me, it is where it all began. This single question has been my best friend, therapist, my career in a sentence, a safe space and my identity for nearly a decade now.

From survivors of human trafficking in Nepal to middle-school children in Afghanistan to refugees in Europe to abandoned ghost villages in Uttarakhand, from women of the Maasai tribe to students in classrooms in Belgium, I have had the privilege to ask this question even at the United Nations Headquarters in New York.

It's not a new story, but at least for this book, I think it's worth sharing again. My mother was pulled out of school in class 5 and was never allowed to study. Growing up, she constantly reminded my sister and I to study hard because we had the opportunity and the resources. I was fascinated seeing that a woman who had not read world literature or solved a maths equation could be so wise and financially proactive in running the house. At the age of fourteen, I asked her how did she know so much when she did not go to school. She replied saying that life was her classroom. Her answer encouraged me to explore that if she was learning simply by living, everyone who is living is learning something. From the next day, I was on a mission to collect as many life lessons as possible. To be honest, it wasn't with the vision of running an organization some day. Rather I wanted to accumulate so much wisdom by the time I turned eighteen that I would become the first person in history to commit no mistakes. When I did turn eighteen, I realized that the power of learning from other people's experiences is not that you don't commit any mistakes but that you avoid the ones that a million others have already committed. The purpose emerged over time, from sharing life lessons with friends over coffee to designing them into experiential modules. My works today derives its strength from producing an opportunity for people like my mother to create an impact. For world curriculums to reflect the stories of everyday people.

People who have never given it a thought ask, 'What is a life lesson?' Tapshi Dhanda, my dear friend and the first editor of Project FUEL's English blog, puts it best: Let me begin by telling you what it is not.

It is not a quote you have read in a book or heard in a movie, or the lyrics of a song, which somehow define your life to a T. It is a lesson your life taught you. You may have learnt it the hard way or the easy way, the long way or the short way, the crystal clear way, the discovering-in-a-haze way, *but the only words that matter here are 'you' and 'learnt'.* You learnt it. You extracted it out of the way(s) life was trying to teach it to you. You pulled it out, examined it and made it your own.

Your life lesson can come to you in one sudden experience, or gradually with introspection, or in hindsight, over months and years. But the fact remains that you learn it all by yourself.

You don't have to live an extraordinary life, or go ahead, live an absolutely extraordinary life; it matters little. What's important is that you live. Wholly. Presently, as much as possible. And mindfully.

All the wealth you accumulate will help secure the future of your next generation. But all the wisdom you document and share will safeguard the life of all your generations that will ever exist. Never underestimate the power a single sentence holds—to revolutionize someone's life, to help someone find a purpose, make peace with this world or heal despite the odds. Your life lesson is a gift to your soul by your being. In its DNA is the story of your existence. Make it count.

The pursuit of my own life lesson, along with that of seven billion people across the world, has served me well so far. It has been my yellow-brick road of blessing, my conversation-starter and, most of all, my North Star to writing this book. Life has taught me, amid other lessons, to share my story. As often as possible, with as many people as possible and as many times as possible. In its sharing, someone will find a connection, a thread to their own story. And this is the hope, right? To be a constellation in a world full of stars.

To a lifetime of learnings.

# Acknowledgements

'Thank you' is a puzzling set of words—abundant yet scarce. Everything and still nothing. Yet, they are all we have to express our deepest gratitude in the simplest and sincerest way.

Although this book is packed with many names that I bow down to with utmost love, there are many more who have stood in the gap, uplifted and helped me each step of the way. I'd like to start by thanking God—the greater force in the universe—who I believe helps me pull through in uncertain times. Mom and Dad, thank you for taking a chance on my dreams despite your humble background and limited financial ability. Your daily heroism, soaring ambitions for your children and continued love has cushioned me against all hardship.

My sister, Deepika—if there were words to describe what you mean to me, I would use them. But for now, I think just saying an honest 'I love you' will suffice. Thank you for listening to my rants, housing my anxiety and keeping my faith alive at all hours. Birendra, for sharing Deepika with me so lovingly.

The joy in my heart rises thinking about Apoorva who is my guardian angel and soul keeper, for the countless nights of advice and guidance across time zones. Rohit, if you had not taken me to that bookstore in San Francisco, perhaps this book would have been delayed by another decade. Thank you to the entire Bakshi clan for helping me earn a family apart from my own.

Aprajita and Avijit, I am grateful to call you two not only my best room-mates and friends but my true siblings.

Tapshi, for always encouraging me to unload my thoughts on paper and reassuring the writer in me to consider that what I have to offer might just be worth it. Thank you, Caspian, for reading the manuscript and giving me your honest feedback with colour-coded inputs. Suhasini, for all the comforting books you have gifted me for getting over the block. Leonardo Capel, for checking in on me and making a pact to write his book while I write mine.

It's not lost on me how much Mehak and Ayushi have taken on the pressure to ease my schedule at work. I am grateful to you both for providing me the space to dream a bigger dream one day at a time.

To my editor, Radhika, thank you for your patience, creativity and big, compassionate smile. I value you for the unwavering faith you deployed in making this book happen. A big shout-out to Rukun for connecting us and being a strong cheerleader. Gunjan, for the beautiful cover, and the Penguin Random House family for including me in your prestigious authors' tribe.

Radhika Dudhat, Priyanka and Mitisha at Shardul Amarchand Mangaldas & Co. for being the most perfect legal counsel I could ask for.

My writing inspirations and role models—Oprah Winfrey, Maya Angelou, Ruskin Bond, Sudha Murty, Khaled Hosseini, Robert Fulghum, Gulzar Sahab, Richard Carlson and Maria Popova. I am indebted. I curled my back to the world with your work, and the bonfire of your artistry never left me cold. Thank you for sharing the gift of your words and wisdom.

From having practically no friends growing up to having so many now that it's hard to name them all, I pass on my love to each one of you for nurturing me with your warmth and joy. My teachers at school, professors in college, friends at the AWWA hostel—for polishing my skills, over the years, of sharing what I know with others. My last and most heartfelt thank you to every person who has been a part of the Project FUEL family, every person who ever had an @projectfuel.in email address, has been a FUEL Fellow, volunteered for our projects, attended our workshops, talks and events, mentored us, clapped for us, contributed to our life lesson database, played the '50 Toughest Questions' game online or offline, or forwarded our message in any capacity.

What an incredible privilege it is to have people around you who are genuinely happy for you.

Until all world languages conspire to invent other words to better express blessings, appreciation, grace and respect, let my thank you be only a glimpse of my gratitude.

# Bibliography

Boreham, F. Goodreads. https://www.goodreads.com/quotes/
9503214-the-eyes-cleansed-by-weeping-have-obtained-
a-clearer-vision (accessed February 13, 2019).

Donne, J. Goodreads. https://www.goodreads.com/quotes/
78366-any-man-s-death-diminishes-me-because-i-am-
involved-in (accessed May 16, 2019).

Emerson, R. Goodreads. https://www.goodreads.com/
quotes/7213675-to-laugh-often-and-much-to-win-the-
respect-of (accessed May 3, 2019).

Koch, R. The Day Will Come When Man Will Have
to Fight Noise As Inexorably As Cholera and the
Plague. Goodreads, https://www.goodreads.com/
quotes/9895691-the-day-will-come-when-man-will-
have-to-fight (accessed May 10, 2019).

Nietzsche, F. Goodreads. https://www.goodreads.com/
quotes/4984-all-truth-is-simple-is-that-not-doubly-a
(accessed May 3, 2019).

Popova, M. Artist Agnes Martin on Inspiration,
Interruptions, Cultivating a Creative Atmosphere, and

the Only Type of Person You Should Allow Into Your Studio. Brainpickings, https://www.brainpickings.org/2016/02/23/agnes-martin-inspiration/ (accessed April 7, 2019).

Popova, M. Brené Brown on Vulnerability, Human Connection, and the Difference Between Empathy and Sympathy, Animated. Brainpickings, https://www.brainpickings.org/2013/12/11/brene-brown-rsa-animated/ (accessed August 5, 2019).

Popova. M., Leo Buscaglia on Education, Industrialized Conformity, and How Stereotypes and Labels Limit Love. Brainpickings, https://www.brainpickings.org/2014/05/19/leo-buscaglia-love-labels/ (accessed February 25, 2019).

Popova, M., Maya Angelou on Identity and Meaning of Life. Brainpickings, https://www.brainpickings.org/2014/05/29/maya-angelou-on-identity-and-the-meaning-of-life/ (accessed April 7, 2019).

Popova, M. Paul Goodman on the Nine Kinds of Silence. Brainpickings, ttps://www.brainpickings.org/2015/01/13/paul-goodman-silence/ (accessed March 12, 2019).

Rilke, R., For The Sake of a Single Poem. Goodreads, https://www.goodreads.com/quotes/9380864-for-the-sake-of-a-single-poem-ah-poems-amount (accessed April 6, 2019).

Rim, J.R. Goodreads. https://www.goodreads.com/quotes/7229285-intelligence-is-what-we-learn-wisdom-is-what-we-unlearn (accessed August 11, 2019).

Toffler, A. Goodreads. https://www.goodreads.com/quotes/8800-the-illiterate-of-the-21st-century-will-not-be-those (accessed March 9, 2019).

Twain, M. Goodreads. https://www.goodreads.com/quotes/
    4957-the-difference-between-the-almost-right-word-
    and-the-right (accessed on October 4, 2019).
Ulrich, L. Ever Widening Circles. https://everwideningcircles.
    com/2015/11/07/maya-angelou-just-do-right/ (accessed
    May 26, 2019).
Usher, S. I Like Words. Letters of Note. https://lettersofnote.
    com/2012/03/13/i-like-words/ (accessed on July 23,
    2019).
Walton, E. The Pervasiveness of Loss. https://steemit.
    com/story/@ericvancewalton/the-pervasiveness-of-loss
    (accessed April 6, 2019).